KT-134-368

© 9/15 I found

EYEWITNESS GUIDES

OCEAN

THIS BOOK BELONGS TO
MR WHITE
If found please contact
mrwhitesbooks@outlook.com

I found

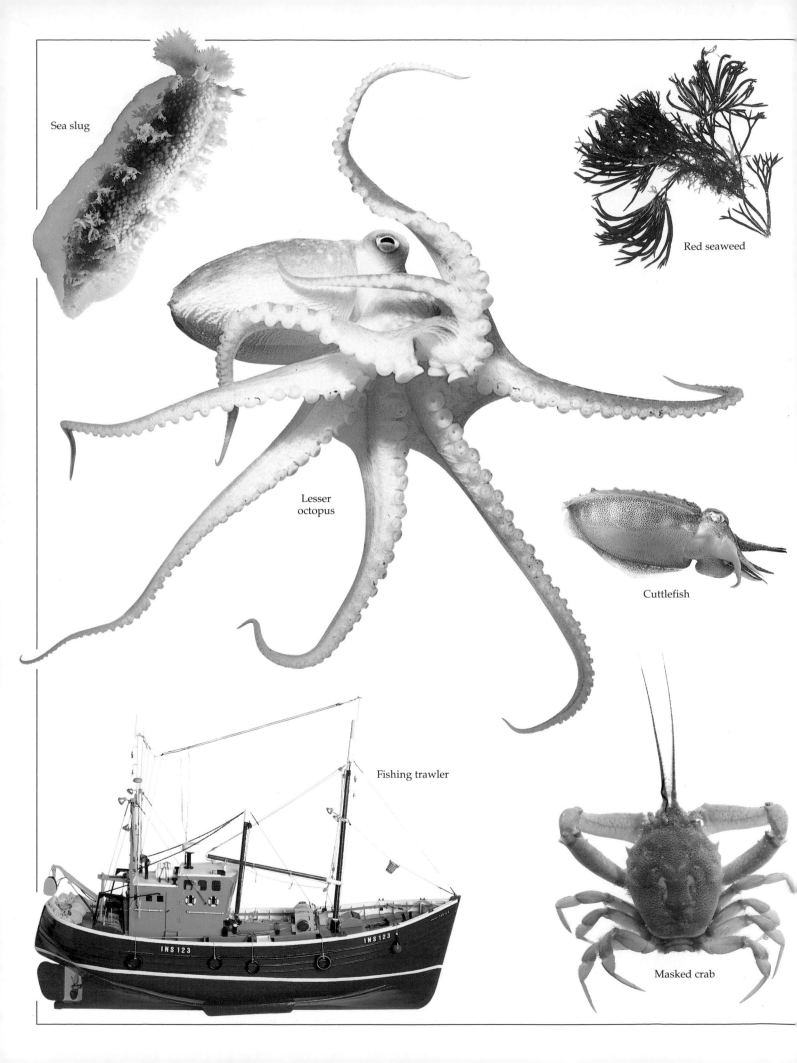

Sea slug

Red seaweed

Lesser
octopus

Cuttlefish

Fishing trawler

INS 123

Masked crab

Boar fish

EYEWITNESS GUIDES

European
spiny lobster

OCEAN

Written by
DR. MIRANDA MACQUITTY

Photographed by
FRANK GREENAWAY

Butterfly blenny

Maerl
seaweed

Common
sea urchin

DORLING KINDERSLEY
London • New York • Stuttgart

Common
starfish

Parchment worm
inside its tube

Red
cushion
star

Mussel shells

Microscope used in
the late 1800s

Red
cushion
star

Prepared slides

Common sunstar

Dead man's
fingers

Bloody
Henry
starfish

Juvenile lumpsucker

Victorian
collection of
shells

Preserving jar
containing a
Norwegian
lobster

A DORLING KINDERSLEY BOOK

Project editor Marion Dent
Art editor Jane Tetzlaff
Managing editor Gillian Denton
Managing art editor Julia Harris
Research Céline Carez
Picture research Kathy Lockley
Production Catherine Semark
Special thanks The University Marine Biological
Station (Scotland) and Sea Life Centres (UK)

This Eyewitness ® Guide has been conceived by
Dorling Kindersley Limited and Editions
Gallimard

First published in Great Britain in 1995 by
Dorling Kindersley Limited,
9 Henrietta Street, London WC2E 8PS

4 6 8 10 9 7 5 3

Copyright © 1995 Dorling Kindersley Limited, London

Visit us on the World Wide Web at
http://www.dk.com

All rights reserved. No part of this publication
may be reproduced, stored in a retrieval system,
or transmitted in any form or by any means,
electronic, mechanical, photocopying, recording
or otherwise, without the prior written
permission of the copyright owner.

A CIP catalogue record for this book is
available from the British Library.

ISBN 0 7513 6056 2

Filmsetting by Litho Link Ltd, Welshpool, Powys
Colour reproduction by Colourscan, Singapore
Printed in China by Toppan Printing Co., (Shenzhen) Ltd

Contents

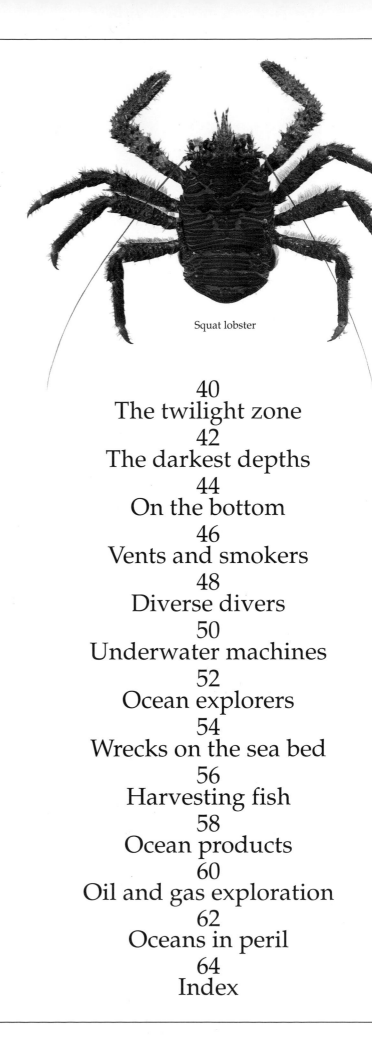

Squat lobster

6
Oceans of the past
8
Oceans today
10
Life in the oceans
12
Waves and weather
14
Sandy and muddy
16
Soft sea bed
18
Rocks underwater
20
On the rocks
22
The coral kingdom
24
Life on a coral reef
26
Sea meadows
28
Predators and prey
30
Homes and hiding
32
Attack and defence
34
The jet set
36
Moving along
38
Ocean travellers

40
The twilight zone
42
The darkest depths
44
On the bottom
46
Vents and smokers
48
Diverse divers
50
Underwater machines
52
Ocean explorers
54
Wrecks on the sea bed
56
Harvesting fish
58
Ocean products
60
Oil and gas exploration
62
Oceans in peril
64
Index

Oceans of the past

THE EARTH, WITH ITS VAST EXPANSES of ocean, has not always looked the way it does today. Over millions of years the land masses have drifted across the face of the earth as new oceans opened up and old oceans have disappeared. Today's oceans only started to take shape in the last 200 million years of the earth's 4,500-million-year existence. But water in the form of vapour was present in the atmosphere of the early earth. As the earth cooled, water vapour condensed making storm clouds from which rain fell and eventually filled the oceans. As the oceans themselves changed, so too did life within the oceans. Simple organisms first appeared in the oceans 3,300 million years ago and were followed by more and more complex life forms. Some forms of life became extinct, but others still survive in the ocean today, more or less unchanged.

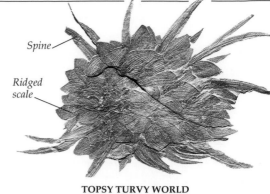

Spine

Ridged scale

TOPSY TURVY WORLD
Wiwaxia lived on the sea floor 530 million years ago, yet this fossil was found high above sea level in Canada's Rocky Mountains. This shows just how much the earth's surface has changed, with land, originally formed under the sea, forced up to form mountain chains.

Strong belly ribs protected under-side of bulky, rounded body

Short tail relative to total body length

Femur, or thigh bone, articulated with pelvic girdle

Huge, long, flat flipper made up of five rows of elongated toes

Arm used for moving and catching food

Fossil brittle star, *Palaeocoma*

STILL HERE TODAY
This 180-million-year-old fossil brittle star looks like its living relative (above). Brittle stars have a round central disc and five, very fragile, jointed arms, that can easily break. Today, as in the past, large numbers are often found on sandy or muddy sea beds.

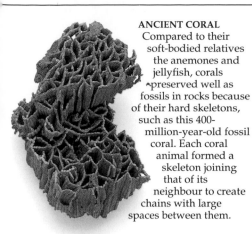

ANCIENT CORAL
Compared to their soft-bodied relatives the anemones and jellyfish, corals preserved well as fossils in rocks because of their hard skeletons, such as this 400-million-year-old fossil coral. Each coral animal formed a skeleton joining that of its neighbour to create chains with large spaces between them.

CHANGING OCEANS
One giant ocean, Panthalassa, surrounded the super-continent Pangaea (1), 290–240 mya (million years ago). At the end of this period, many kinds of marine life became extinct. Pangaea broke up, with part drifting north and part south, with the Tethys Sea between.

CONTINENTAL DRIFT
The northern part split to form the North Atlantic 208–146 mya (2). The South Atlantic and Indian Oceans began to form 146–65 mya (3). The continents continued to drift 1.64 mya (4). Today the oceans are still changing shape – the Atlantic Ocean gets wider by a few centimetres each year.

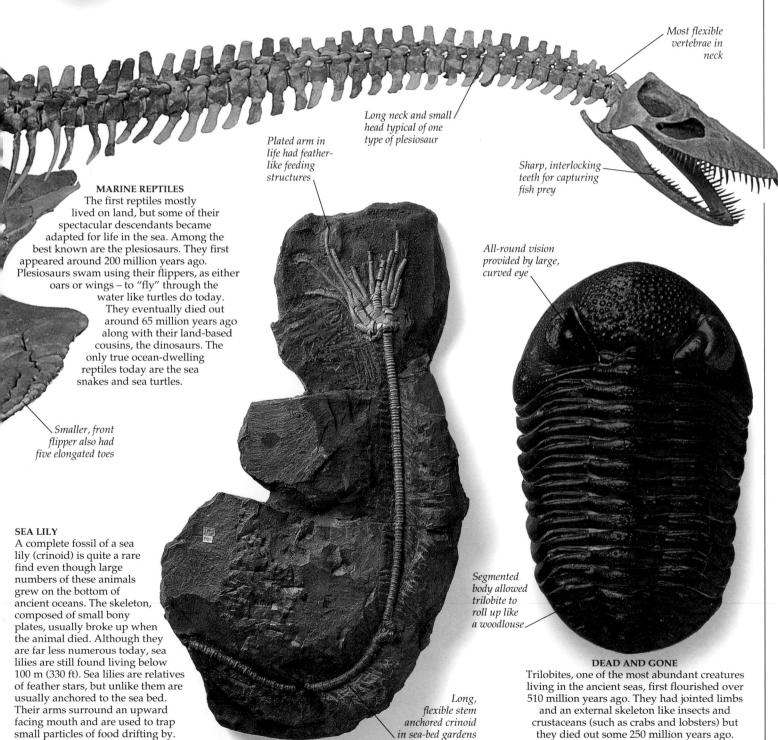

Most flexible vertebrae in neck

Long neck and small head typical of one type of plesiosaur

Plated arm in life had feather-like feeding structures

Sharp, interlocking teeth for capturing fish prey

MARINE REPTILES
The first reptiles mostly lived on land, but some of their spectacular descendants became adapted for life in the sea. Among the best known are the plesiosaurs. They first appeared around 200 million years ago. Plesiosaurs swam using their flippers, as either oars or wings – to "fly" through the water like turtles do today. They eventually died out around 65 million years ago along with their land-based cousins, the dinosaurs. The only true ocean-dwelling reptiles today are the sea snakes and sea turtles.

All-round vision provided by large, curved eye

Smaller, front flipper also had five elongated toes

SEA LILY
A complete fossil of a sea lily (crinoid) is quite a rare find even though large numbers of these animals grew on the bottom of ancient oceans. The skeleton, composed of small bony plates, usually broke up when the animal died. Although they are far less numerous today, sea lilies are still found living below 100 m (330 ft). Sea lilies are relatives of feather stars, but unlike them are usually anchored to the sea bed. Their arms surround an upward facing mouth and are used to trap small particles of food drifting by.

Segmented body allowed trilobite to roll up like a woodlouse

Long, flexible stem anchored crinoid in sea-bed gardens

DEAD AND GONE
Trilobites, one of the most abundant creatures living in the ancient seas, first flourished over 510 million years ago. They had jointed limbs and an external skeleton like insects and crustaceans (such as crabs and lobsters) but they died out some 250 million years ago.

Oceans today

Leafy sea
dragon

Dip a toe in any ocean and you are linked to all the world's oceans as the earth's sea water is one continuous mass. The largest expanses are called oceans while the smaller ones (usually close to, or partly enclosed by, land) are called seas. Two-thirds of the earth's surface is covered by sea water which makes up to 97 per cent of the planet's entire water supply. Sea water's temperature varies in different areas – it is colder at the surface in polar regions than in the tropics. Generally, sea water gets colder with depth. Sea water's salinity varies from that of the saltiest waters (such as the desert-bound Red Sea where there is a high evaporation rate and little inflow of freshwater) to one of the least salty (the Baltic Sea where there is a high inflow of freshwater from rivers). Nor is the bottom of the ocean the same everywhere. There are undersea mountains, plateaus, plains, and trenches, making the ocean floor as complex as any geological formations on land.

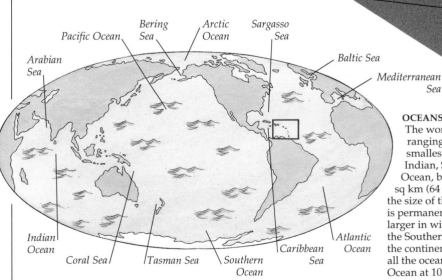

Haiti/Dominican Republic

Sea level

Tobago

Trinidad

North coast of Venezuela

South America

Georgetown (capital of Guyana)

Continental Shelf

Guiana Plateau

Continental Slope

Model (right) of a section of the sea floor east of the Caribbean, as shown in red square on map (below)

Bering Sea

Arctic Ocean

Sargasso Sea

Pacific Ocean

Arabian Sea

Baltic Sea

Mediterranean Sea

Indian Ocean

Coral Sea

Tasman Sea

Southern Ocean

Caribbean Sea

Atlantic Ocean

OCEANS OF OCEANS
The world's five oceans, ranging from the largest to the smallest, are the Pacific, Atlantic, Indian, Southern, and Arctic. The Pacific Ocean, by far the largest, covers 166 million sq km (64 million sq miles) and is about 13 times the size of the Arctic Ocean. The Arctic Ocean's centre is permanently covered by a layer of sea ice which grows larger in winter and shrinks in summer by melting. Over half the Southern Ocean is also frozen in winter and sea ice still fringes the continent of Antarctica during the summer. The average depth of all the oceans is 3,650 m (12,000 ft) with the deepest part in the Pacific Ocean at 10,920 m (36,000 ft) in the Mariana Trench, east of the Philippines.

SEA OR LAKE?
The water in the Dead Sea is saltier than any ocean because the water that drains into it evaporates in the hot sun, leaving behind the salts. A body is more buoyant in such salty water, making it easier to float. The Dead Sea is a lake, not a sea, because it is completely surrounded by land. True seas are always connected to the ocean by a channel.

Floating on the
Dead Sea

GOD OF THE WATERS
Neptune, the Roman god of the sea, is usually shown riding a dolphin and carrying a pronged spear (trident). It was thought he also controlled freshwater supplies, so offerings were made to him at the driest time of the year.

Hatteras Abyssal Plain

Puerto Rico Trench

Nares Abyssal Plain

DISAPPEARING ACT
The gigantic plates on the earth's crust move like a conveyor belt. As new areas of ocean floor form at spreading centres, old areas disappear into the molten heart of the planet. This diagram shows one oceanic plate being forced under another (subduction) in the Mariana Trench, creating an island arc.

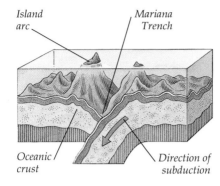

Island arc

Mariana Trench

Oceanic crust

Direction of subduction

Formation of Mariana Trench

Mid-Atlantic Ridge

Kane Fracture Zone

THE OCEAN FLOOR
This model shows the features on the bottom of the Atlantic Ocean off the northeast coast of South America from Guyana to Venezuela. Off this coast is the Continental Shelf, a region of relatively shallow water about 200 m (660 ft) deep. Here the Continental Shelf is about 200 km (125 miles) wide, but off the coast of northern Asia it is as much as 1,600 km (1,000 miles) wide. At the outer edge of the Continental Shelf, the ocean floor drops away steeply to form the Continental Slope. Sediments eroded from the land and carried by rivers, such as the Orinoco, accumulate at the bottom of this Continental Slope. The ocean floor then opens out in virtually flat areas (abyssal plains), which are covered with a deep layer of soft sediments. The Puerto Rican Trench formed where one of the earth's plates (the North American Plate) is sliding past another (the Caribbean Plate). An arc of volcanic islands have also been created where the North American Plate is forced under the Caribbean Plate. The fracture zones are offsets of the Mid-Atlantic Ridge.

Vema Fracture Zone

Demerara Abyssal Plain

Life in the oceans

F ROM THE SEA SHORE to the deepest depths, oceans are home to some of the most diverse life on earth. Animals live either on the sea bed or in mid-water where they swim or float. Plants are only found in the sunlit zone where there is enough light for them to grow either anchored to the bottom or drifting in the water. Animals are found at all depths of the oceans, but are most abundant in the sunlit zone where food is plentiful. Not all free-swimming animals stay in one zone – the sperm whale dives to over 500 m (1,650 ft) to feed on squid, returning to the surface to breathe air. Some animals from cold, deep waters, such as the Greenland shark in the Atlantic, are also found in the cold, surface waters of polar regions. Over 90 per cent of all species dwell on the bottom. One rock can be home to at least ten major types, such as corals, molluscs, and sponges. Most ocean animals and plants have their origins in the sea, but some like whales and sea grasses are descended from ancestors that once lived on land.

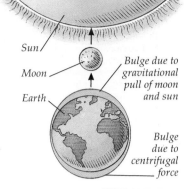

Sun

Moon

Earth

Bulge due to gravitational pull of moon and sun

Bulge due to centrifugal force

TIME AND TIDE
Anyone spending time by the seaside or in an estuary will notice the tides. Tides are caused by the gravitational pull of the moon on the earth's mass of seawater. An equal and opposite bulge of water occurs on the side of the earth away from the moon, due to centrifugal force. As the earth spins on its axis, the bulges (high tides) usually occur twice a day in any one place. The highest and lowest tides occur when the moon and sun are in line causing the greatest gravitational pull. These are the spring tides at new and full moon.

Bloody Henry starfish

Common sunstar

SHORE LIFE
Often found on the shore at low tide, starfish also live in deeper water. Sea life on the shore must either be tough enough to withstand drying out, or shelter in rock pools. The toughest animals and plants live high on the shore, but the least able to cope in air are found at the bottom.

SQUISHY SQUID
Squid are among the most common animals living in the ocean. Like fish, they often swim around in shoals for protection in numbers. Their torpedo-shaped bodies are streamlined so they can swim fast.

Inside squid's soft body is a horny, pen-like shell

Tentacles reach out to grasp food

Deep-sea cat shark grows to only 50 cm (20 in) long

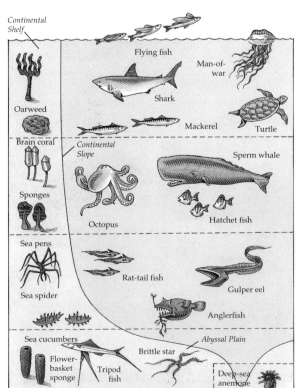

Note: Neither the marine life or zones are drawn to scale

Sunlit Zone
0–200 m
(0–660 ft)

Twilight Zone
200–1,000 m
(660–3,300 ft)

Dark Zone
1,000–4,000 m
(3,300–13,200 ft)

Abyss
4,000–6,000 m
(13,200–19,800 ft)

Trench
Over 6,000 m
(19,800 ft)

Continental Shelf

Flying fish

Man-of-war

Shark

Oarweed

Mackerel

Turtle

Brain coral

Continental Slope

Sperm whale

Sponges

Octopus

Hatchet fish

Sea pens

Sea spider

Rat-tail fish

Gulper eel

Anglerfish

Sea cucumbers

Abyssal Plain

Flower-basket sponge

Brittle star

Tripod fish

Deep-sea anemone

THE OCEAN'S ZONES
The ocean is divided up into broad zones, according to how far down sunlight penetrates and the water temperature. In the Sunlit Zone, there is plenty of light, much water movement, and seasonal changes in temperature. Beneath this is the Twilight Zone, the maximum depth where light penetrates. Temperatures here decrease rapidly with depth to about 5°C (41°F). Deeper yet is the Dark Zone, where there is no light and temperatures drop to about 1–2°C (34–36°F). Still in darkness and even deeper is the Abyss and then the Trenches. There are also zones on the sea bed. The shallowest zone ranges from the low tide mark to the edge of the Continental Shelf. Below this are the Continental Slope and finally the Abyssal Plains.

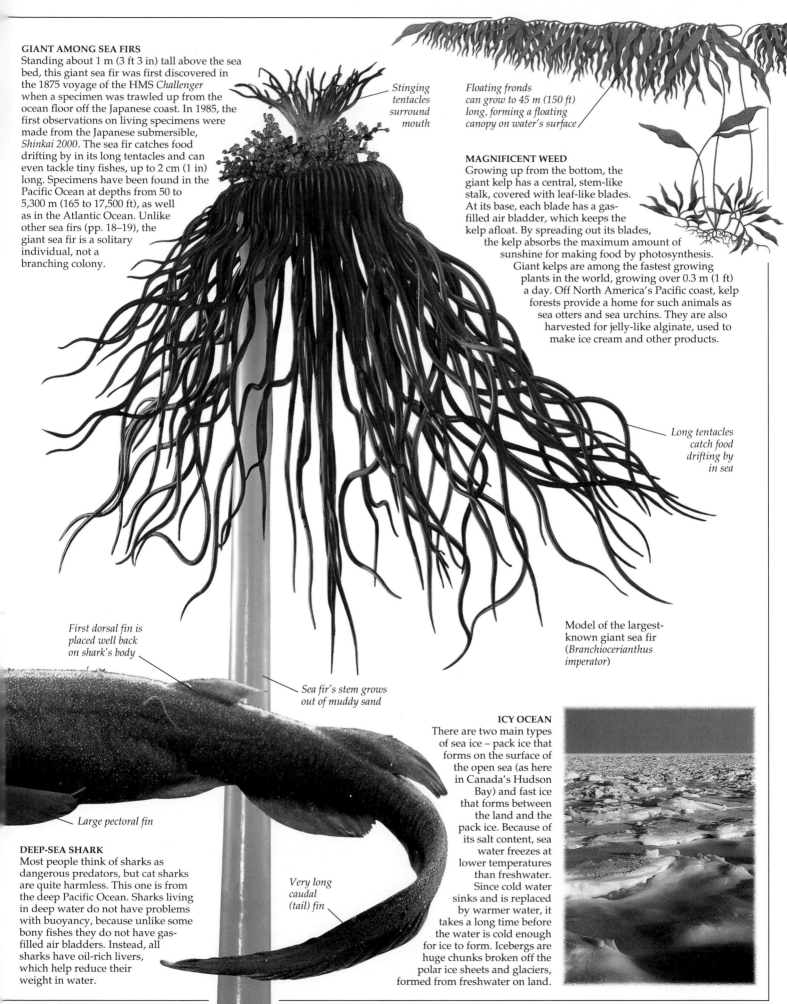

GIANT AMONG SEA FIRS

Standing about 1 m (3 ft 3 in) tall above the sea bed, this giant sea fir was first discovered in the 1875 voyage of the HMS *Challenger* when a specimen was trawled up from the ocean floor off the Japanese coast. In 1985, the first observations on living specimens were made from the Japanese submersible, *Shinkai 2000*. The sea fir catches food drifting by in its long tentacles and can even tackle tiny fishes, up to 2 cm (1 in) long. Specimens have been found in the Pacific Ocean at depths from 50 to 5,300 m (165 to 17,500 ft), as well as in the Atlantic Ocean. Unlike other sea firs (pp. 18–19), the giant sea fir is a solitary individual, not a branching colony.

Stinging tentacles surround mouth

Floating fronds can grow to 45 m (150 ft) long, forming a floating canopy on water's surface

MAGNIFICENT WEED

Growing up from the bottom, the giant kelp has a central, stem-like stalk, covered with leaf-like blades. At its base, each blade has a gas-filled air bladder, which keeps the kelp afloat. By spreading out its blades, the kelp absorbs the maximum amount of sunshine for making food by photosynthesis. Giant kelps are among the fastest growing plants in the world, growing over 0.3 m (1 ft) a day. Off North America's Pacific coast, kelp forests provide a home for such animals as sea otters and sea urchins. They are also harvested for jelly-like alginate, used to make ice cream and other products.

Long tentacles catch food drifting by in sea

First dorsal fin is placed well back on shark's body

Sea fir's stem grows out of muddy sand

Model of the largest-known giant sea fir (Branchiocerianthus imperator)

Large pectoral fin

DEEP-SEA SHARK

Most people think of sharks as dangerous predators, but cat sharks are quite harmless. This one is from the deep Pacific Ocean. Sharks living in deep water do not have problems with buoyancy, because unlike some bony fishes they do not have gas-filled air bladders. Instead, all sharks have oil-rich livers, which help reduce their weight in water.

Very long caudal (tail) fin

ICY OCEAN

There are two main types of sea ice – pack ice that forms on the surface of the open sea (as here in Canada's Hudson Bay) and fast ice that forms between the land and the pack ice. Because of its salt content, sea water freezes at lower temperatures than freshwater. Since cold water sinks and is replaced by warmer water, it takes a long time before the water is cold enough for ice to form. Icebergs are huge chunks broken off the polar ice sheets and glaciers, formed from freshwater on land.

Waves and weather

Sea water is constantly moving. At the surface, wind-driven waves can be 15 m (50 ft) troughs. Major surface currents are driven by the prevailing winds, including trade winds that blow towards the equator. Both surface and deep-water currents help modify the world's climate by taking cold water from the polar regions towards the tropics, and vice versa. Shifts in this flow affect life in the ocean. In an El Niño (climate change), warm water starts to flow down the west of South America which stops nutrient-rich, cold water rising up, causing plankton and fisheries to fail. Heat from oceans creates air movement, from swirling hurricanes to day-time breezes on-shore, or night-time ones off-shore. Breezes occur as the ocean heats up more slowly than the land in the day. Cool air above the water blows in, replacing warm air above the land, and the reverse at night.

DOWN THE SPOUT
Water spouts (spinning sprays sucked up from the surface) begin when whirling air drops down from a storm cloud to the ocean.

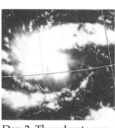

Day 2: Thunderstorms as swirling cloud mass

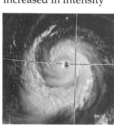

Day 4: Winds have increased in intensity

Day 7: Strong winds

A HURRICANE IS BORN
These satellite photographs show a hurricane developing. On day 2 a swirling cloud mass is formed. By day 4 fierce winds develop about the centre. By day 7 winds are the strongest.

RIVERS OF THE SEA
Currents are huge masses of water moving through the oceans. The course currents follow is not precisely the same as the trade winds and westerlies, because currents are deflected by land and the Coriolis Force produced by the earth's rotation. The latter causes currents to shift to the right in the northern hemisphere and to the left in the southern. There are also currents which flow due to differences in density of sea water.

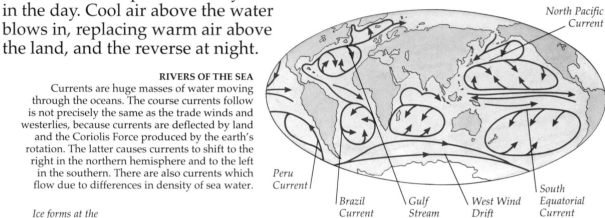

North Pacific Current

Peru Current

Brazil Current

Gulf Stream

West Wind Drift

South Equatorial Current

Ice forms at the very top of the clouds

Hurricanes are enormous – some may be 800 km (480 miles) across

Warm, moist air spirals up around the eye inside the hurricane

Torrential rains fall from clouds

Energy to drive storm comes from warm ocean at 27°C (80°F) or more

HEART OF A HURRICANE
Hurricanes (also known as typhoons) are the most destructive forces created by the oceans. They develop in the tropics where warm, moist air rises up from the ocean's surface creating storm clouds. As more air spirals upwards, energy is released, fuelling stronger winds which whirl around the eye (a calm area of extreme low pressure). Hurricanes move onto land and cause terrible devastation. Away from the ocean, hurricanes die out.

Strongest winds of up to 360 kph (220 mph) occur just outside the eye

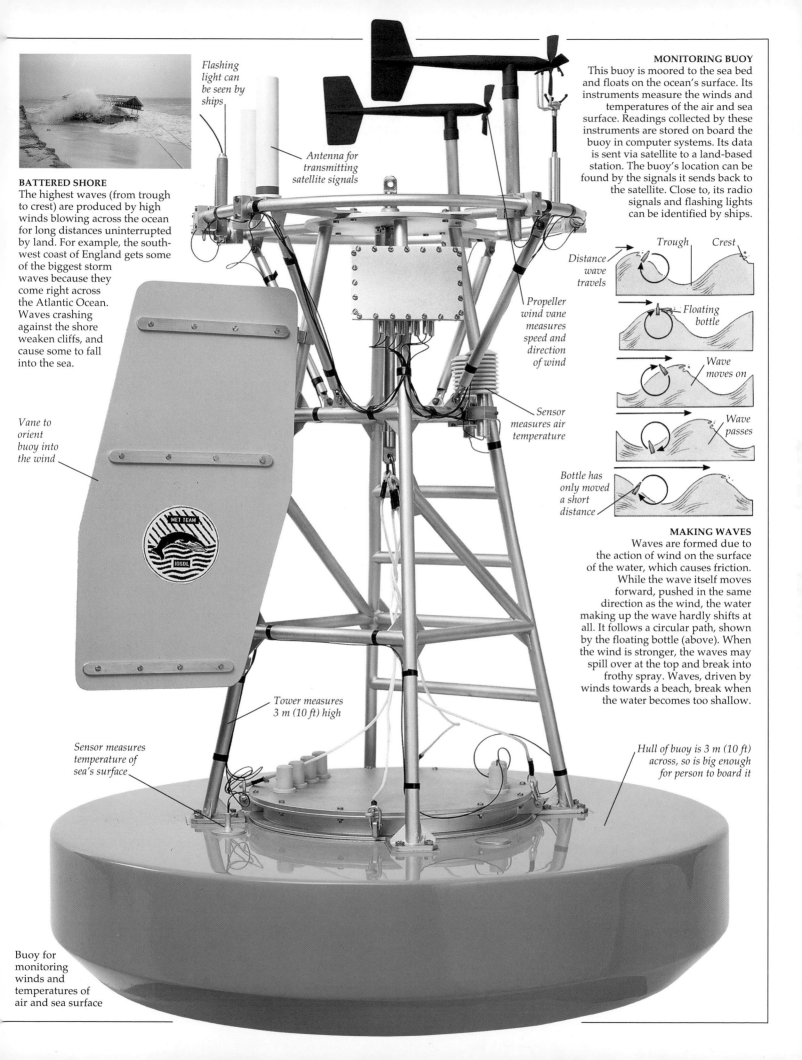

BATTERED SHORE

The highest waves (from trough to crest) are produced by high winds blowing across the ocean for long distances uninterrupted by land. For example, the south-west coast of England gets some of the biggest storm waves because they come right across the Atlantic Ocean. Waves crashing against the shore weaken cliffs, and cause some to fall into the sea.

Flashing light can be seen by ships

Antenna for transmitting satellite signals

MONITORING BUOY

This buoy is moored to the sea bed and floats on the ocean's surface. Its instruments measure the winds and temperatures of the air and sea surface. Readings collected by these instruments are stored on board the buoy in computer systems. Its data is sent via satellite to a land-based station. The buoy's location can be found by the signals it sends back to the satellite. Close to, its radio signals and flashing lights can be identified by ships.

Distance wave travels — *Trough* — *Crest*

Floating bottle

Wave moves on

Wave passes

Bottle has only moved a short distance

Vane to orient buoy into the wind

Propeller wind vane measures speed and direction of wind

Sensor measures air temperature

MAKING WAVES

Waves are formed due to the action of wind on the surface of the water, which causes friction. While the wave itself moves forward, pushed in the same direction as the wind, the water making up the wave hardly shifts at all. It follows a circular path, shown by the floating bottle (above). When the wind is stronger, the waves may spill over at the top and break into frothy spray. Waves, driven by winds towards a beach, break when the water becomes too shallow.

MET TEAM
IOSDL

Tower measures 3 m (10 ft) high

Sensor measures temperature of sea's surface

Hull of buoy is 3 m (10 ft) across, so is big enough for person to board it

Buoy for monitoring winds and temperatures of air and sea surface

Sandy and muddy

IN SHALLOW COASTAL WATERS, from the lowest part of the shore to the edge of the continental shelf, sand and mud are washed from the land, creating vast stretches of sea floor which look like underwater deserts. Finer-grained mud settles in places where the water is calmer. Without rocks, there are no abundant growths of seaweeds, so animals that venture onto the surface are exposed to predators. Many of the creatures avoid them by hiding in the soft sea bed. Some worms hide inside their own tubes, but they can feed by spreading out a fan of tentacles or by drawing water containing food particles into their tubes. Other worms, such as the sea mouse, move around in search of food. Flat fish, like the flounder, are commonly found on the sandy sea bed, looking for any readily available food, such as peacock worms. All the animals shown here live in the coastal waters of the Atlantic Ocean.

Tough papery tube protects soft worm inside

Worm can grow up to 40 cm (16 in) long

Bulky body covered by dense mat of fine hairs

Coarse, shiny bristles help it to move along sea bed

BEAUTIFUL BRISTLE WORM
The sea mouse ploughs its way through muddy sand on the sea bed and is often washed up on the beach after storms. The shiny, rainbow-coloured spines help propel it along and may make this chunky worm less appetizing to fish. The sea mouse usually keeps its rear end out of the sand to bring in a stream of fresh sea water to help it breathe. Sea mice grow to 10 cm (4 in) long and eat any dead animals they may find in the sand.

Light colour helps it merge into sand

Thick trunk looks like a peanut, when whole body retracts

Surface of plump, unsegmented body feels rough

Poisonous spines on first dorsal fin

PEANUT WORM
Many different groups of worms live in the sea. This is one of the sipunculid worms, sometimes called peanut worms. A stretchy front part can retract into the thicker trunk. Peanut worms usually burrow in sand and mud, but some of these 320 different kinds of worm live in empty sea shells and in coral crevices.

Front part can also retract

Poisonous spine on front of gill cover

High-set eye allows all-round vision

Mouth surrounded by tentacles

WARY WEEVER
When a weever fish is buried in sand, its eyes on top of its head help it see what is going on. The weever's strategically-placed poisonous spines provide it with extra defence. The spines can inflict nasty wounds on humans, if a weever is accidentally trodden on in shallow water or caught in fishermen's nets.

FLAT FISH
Flounders cruise along the sea bed looking for food. They can nibble the tops off peacock worms, if they are quick enough to catch them.

Feeler-like palps (sense organs)

Fan-shaped flaps beat to let food pass along worm's body

Parapodia, or feet-like flaps

Parapodia

Red seaweed grows on whitish ends of tube

Tentacle, extended in water, used for feeding and breathing

Mouth

Parchment worm outside its tube

Fan-shaped flap

When buried, the tube is often U-shaped

A LOOK INSIDE
This bizarre looking worm lives in a U-shaped tube that sticks out above the mud's surface. The worm feeds by drawing water containing food into its tube. Fan-shaped flaps in the middle of the worm's body create a water current. Food is trapped in a slimy net which is rolled up and passed towards the mouth at the front of the body. A new net is then made and the process repeated. At night this worm can eject a cloud of glowing material from its burrow, perhaps to ward off predators.

Tentacles disappear fast into tube, if danger is present

LIKE A PEACOCK'S FAN
With their crown of tentacles, peacock worms look like plants, not animals. To help them feed and breathe, tiny hairs on the tentacles' fine fringes create a water current which passes through the crown. Particles in this current are passed down rows of beating hairs into the mouth in the crown's centre. Larger particles, such as sand grains, are not eaten but help make the tube instead.

Peacock worm can be 25 cm (10 in) long

Tube made of mud and sand bound together with worm's hardened slime

Soft sea bed

SWIMMING OVER a soft sea bed, using a mask and snorkel, it is possible to see only a few animals because most of them live buried in the sand. Look closely and you may see signs of buried life (a crab's feathery antennae or a clam's siphon), which help these animals get a clean supply of water containing oxygen to breathe. Some fish, like the eagle ray, visit the soft sea bed to feed on burrowing clams. Other animals are found only where sea grasses grow on sandy bottoms. Sea grasses are not seaweeds but flowering plants. They are food for many animals including the dugong – the only plant-eating mammal that truly lives in the sea.

Tough skin protects dugong

DOCILE DUGONG
Dugongs live in shallow tropical waters where they feed on sea grasses growing in the soft sea bed. They often dig down into the sand to eat the food-rich roots of sea grasses. These gentle, shy animals are still hunted in some places.

Anemone-like polyp unfurls when feeding

SHELL BOAT
In Botticelli's *The Birth of Venus*, the Roman goddess rises from the water in a scallop shell. In real life, scallop shells are too heavy to float and much too small to carry a person.

ELEGANT PEN
Looking like an old-fashioned quill pen, this relative of sea anemones lives in the soft sea bed. The rows of tiny polyps which come out on each side of its body are used to capture small animals drifting by for food. Sea pens glow in the dark if disturbed. Some sea pens grow on the bottom of the deep ocean.

This sea pen can grow to 20 cm (8 in) in height

Long dorsal fin runs along almost whole length of body

RED BAND FISH
This fish usually lives in burrows in the soft sea bed, down to depths of about 200 m (660 ft). It is also found swimming among sea grasses. Sometimes red band fish are found washed up on the beach after storms. When out of its burrow, the fish swims by passing waves down its body. It feeds on small animals drifting by.

Long anal fin

Red band fish may grow to 70 cm (28 in) in length

Stem of sea pen anchors in sandy sea bed

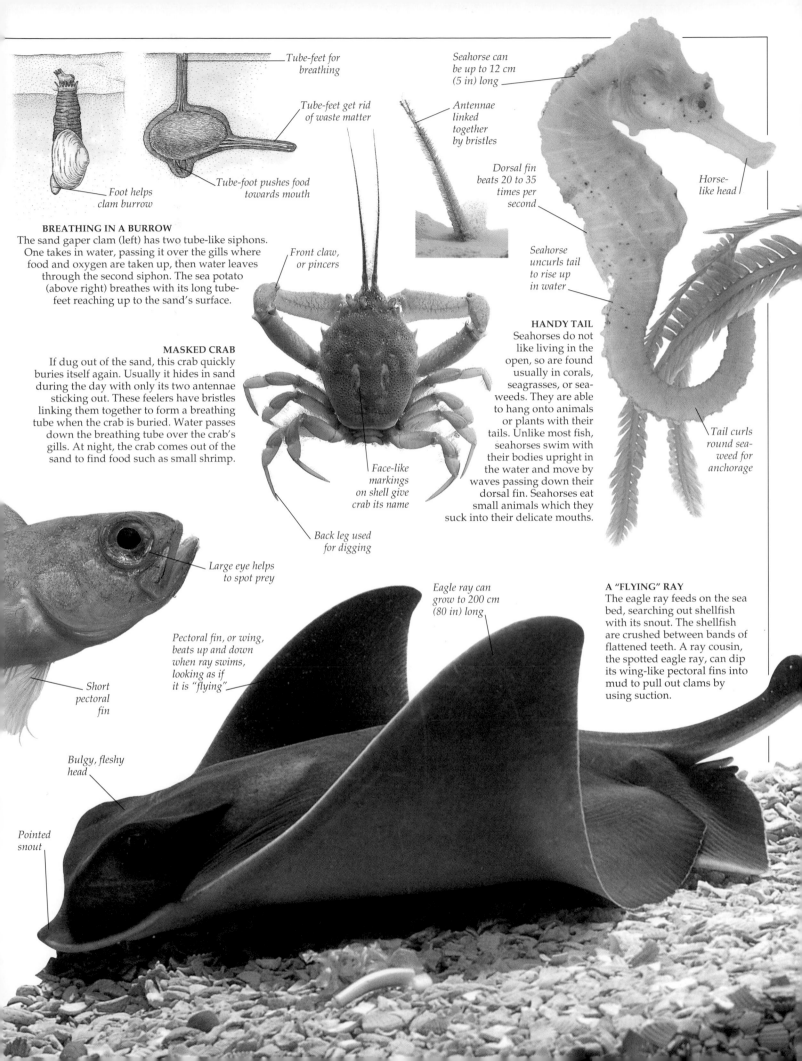

Tube-feet for breathing

Tube-feet get rid of waste matter

Tube-foot pushes food towards mouth

Foot helps clam burrow

Seahorse can be up to 12 cm (5 in) long

Antennae linked together by bristles

Dorsal fin beats 20 to 35 times per second

Horse-like head

BREATHING IN A BURROW
The sand gaper clam (left) has two tube-like siphons. One takes in water, passing it over the gills where food and oxygen are taken up, then water leaves through the second siphon. The sea potato (above right) breathes with its long tube-feet reaching up to the sand's surface.

Front claw, or pincers

Seahorse uncurls tail to rise up in water

HANDY TAIL
Seahorses do not like living in the open, so are found usually in corals, seagrasses, or sea-weeds. They are able to hang onto animals or plants with their tails. Unlike most fish, seahorses swim with their bodies upright in the water and move by waves passing down their dorsal fin. Seahorses eat small animals which they suck into their delicate mouths.

Tail curls round sea-weed for anchorage

MASKED CRAB
If dug out of the sand, this crab quickly buries itself again. Usually it hides in sand during the day with only its two antennae sticking out. These feelers have bristles linking them together to form a breathing tube when the crab is buried. Water passes down the breathing tube over the crab's gills. At night, the crab comes out of the sand to find food such as small shrimp.

Face-like markings on shell give crab its name

Back leg used for digging

Large eye helps to spot prey

Eagle ray can grow to 200 cm (80 in) long

A "FLYING" RAY
The eagle ray feeds on the sea bed, searching out shellfish with its snout. The shellfish are crushed between bands of flattened teeth. A ray cousin, the spotted eagle ray, can dip its wing-like pectoral fins into mud to pull out clams by using suction.

Pectoral fin, or wing, beats up and down when ray swims, looking as if it is "flying"

Short pectoral fin

Bulgy, fleshy head

Pointed snout

Rocks underwater

ROCKS MAKE UP THE SEA BED in coastal waters, where currents sweep away any sand and mud. With the strong water movement, animals must cling onto rocks, find crevices to hide in, or shelter in seaweeds. A few remarkable animals, such as the piddocks (clams) and some sea urchins, can bore into solid rock to make their homes. Sea urchins bore cavities in hard rock while piddocks drill into softer rocks such as sandstone and chalk. Some animals hide under small stones, but only if they are lodged in the soft sea bed. Where masses of loose pebbles roll around, animals and seaweeds can be crushed. However, some crustaceans, such as lobsters, can regrow a lost limb crushed by a stone and starfish can regrow a missing arm. Some animals can survive on the seashore's lower levels, especially rock pools, but many need to be continually submerged.

Sea urchin boring into rocks

Piddock

ROCK BORERS
Some sea urchins use their spines and teeth beneath their shells to bore spaces in rock, while piddocks drill with the tips of their shells. Using its muscular foot, the piddock twists and turns to drill and hold onto its burrow. Both are found in shallow water and on the lower shore.

Dorsal fin has eyespot to frighten predators

BEAUTIFUL BUTTERFLY
Blennies, small fishes living in shallow water, often rest on the bottom and hide in crannies. They lay their eggs in sheltered places, such as abandoned bottles, and guard them from predators. Blennies feed on small creatures, such as mites, and live on rocky or stony ground to depths of 20 m (66 ft).

Spiny shell helps deter predators

SPINY LOBSTER
European spiny lobsters, or crawfish, are reddish-brown in life. With their small pincers, spiny lobsters are restricted to eating soft prey such as worms, or devouring dead animals. They live among rocks, hiding in crevices during the day, but venture out over the sea bed to find food at night. Some kinds of spiny lobsters move in long lines keeping touch with the lobster in front with their antennae.

Delicate claw on tip of walking leg

European spiny lobster, also known as a crawfish

Leg used for walking

Tail can be flapped so lobster can swim backwards

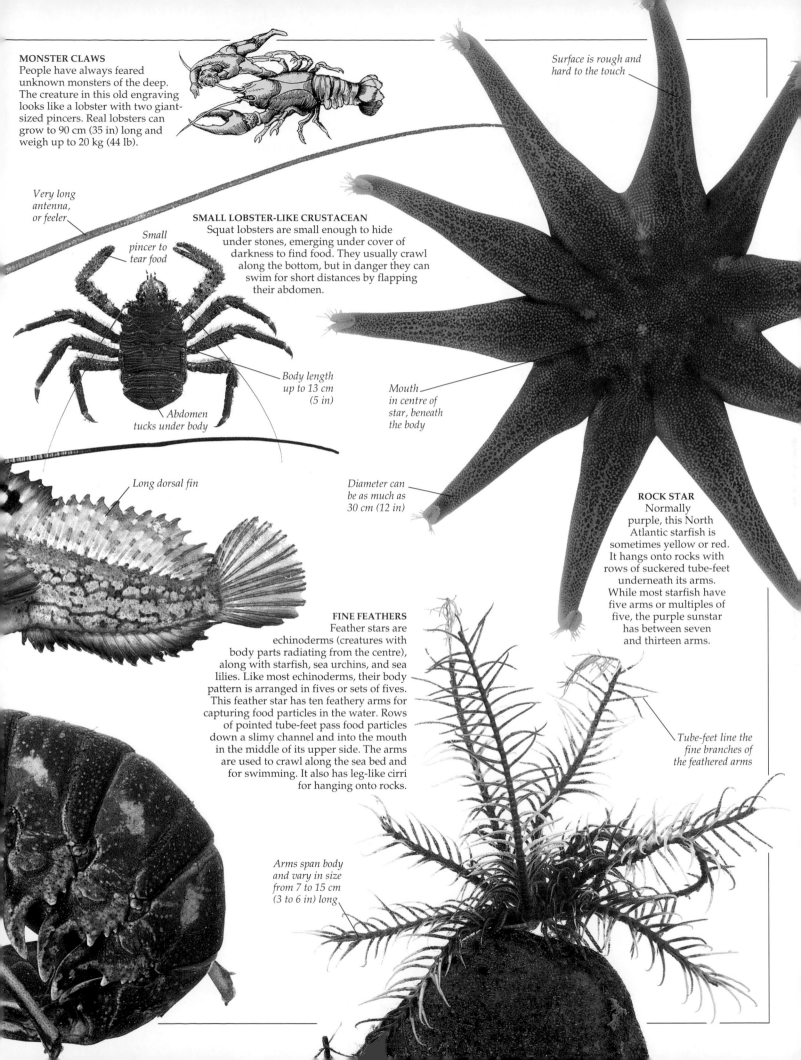

MONSTER CLAWS
People have always feared unknown monsters of the deep. The creature in this old engraving looks like a lobster with two giant-sized pincers. Real lobsters can grow to 90 cm (35 in) long and weigh up to 20 kg (44 lb).

Surface is rough and hard to the touch

Very long antenna, or feeler

Small pincer to tear food

SMALL LOBSTER-LIKE CRUSTACEAN
Squat lobsters are small enough to hide under stones, emerging under cover of darkness to find food. They usually crawl along the bottom, but in danger they can swim for short distances by flapping their abdomen.

Body length up to 13 cm (5 in)

Abdomen tucks under body

Mouth in centre of star, beneath the body

Long dorsal fin

Diameter can be as much as 30 cm (12 in)

ROCK STAR
Normally purple, this North Atlantic starfish is sometimes yellow or red. It hangs onto rocks with rows of suckered tube-feet underneath its arms. While most starfish have five arms or multiples of five, the purple sunstar has between seven and thirteen arms.

FINE FEATHERS
Feather stars are echinoderms (creatures with body parts radiating from the centre), along with starfish, sea urchins, and sea lilies. Like most echinoderms, their body pattern is arranged in fives or sets of fives. This feather star has ten feathery arms for capturing food particles in the water. Rows of pointed tube-feet pass food particles down a slimy channel and into the mouth in the middle of its upper side. The arms are used to crawl along the sea bed and for swimming. It also has leg-like cirri for hanging onto rocks.

Tube-feet line the fine branches of the feathered arms

Arms span body and vary in size from 7 to 15 cm (3 to 6 in) long

On the rocks

IN SHALLOW, COOL WATERS above rocky sea beds, forests of kelp (large brown seaweeds) are home for many animals. Fish swim among the giant fronds. Along North America's Pacific coast, sea otters wrap themselves in kelp while asleep on the surface. Tightly gripping the rocks, the kelp's root-like anchor (holdfast) houses hordes of tiny creatures, such as worms and mites. Unlike the roots of land plants, kelp's holdfast is only an anchor and does not absorb water or nutrients. Other animals grow on the kelp's surface or directly on the rocks and capture food brought to them in the currents. Sea firs look like plants, but are animals belonging to the same group as sea anemones, jellyfish, and corals, and all have stinging tentacles. Anchored to rocks, mussels provide homes for some animals between or within their shells.

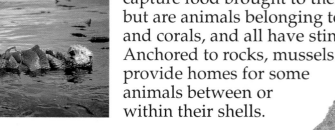

A type of brown seaweed (kelp) found in the Pacific Ocean

DELIGHTFUL MARINE MAMMAL
Sea otters swim and rest among giant kelp fronds along North America's Pacific coast. They dive down to the sea bed to pick up shellfish, smashing them open by banging them against a rock balanced on their chest.

ANCHORED ALGAE
Holdfasts of the large, tough, brown algae called kelp keep it firmly anchored to the rocks. Growing in shallow water, kelp is often battered by waves.

Holdfast of oarweed kelp

Holdfast must be strong, as some kinds of kelp can grow tens of metres long

Scaleless body is covered with small warty bumps

PRETTY BABY
Young lumpsuckers are more beautiful than their dumpy parents which cling onto rocks with sucker-like fins on their bellies. The adult lumpsuckers come into shallow water to breed and the father guards the eggs.

Juvenile lumpsucker

Each sturdy, blunt finger measures at least 3 cm (1.25 in) across

Fleshy fingers supported by many, tiny, hard splinters

White, anemone-like polyp captures food from fast-moving currents

DEAD MAN'S FINGERS
When this soft coral is washed up on the shore, its rubbery, fleshy form lives up to its name! Growing on rocks, the colonies consist of many polyps (feeding heads) within a fleshy, orange or white base.

Gills

SEA MAT
The lacy-looking growth on the kelp's surface (left) is a bryozoan, or moss animal. They live in colonies where many individuals grow next to each other. Each little compartment houses one of these animals, which come out to feed, capturing food in their tiny tentacles. The colony grows as individuals bud off new individuals. Other kinds of moss animal grow upwards, looking like seaweeds or corals. Between the sea mats, a blue-rayed limpet grazes on the kelp's surface.

SEA SLUG
Many sea slugs are meat eaters. This slug lives on the soft coral known as Dead man's fingers. Some sea slugs are able to eat the stinging tentacles of anemones and keep the stings for their own protection. Sea slug eggs hatch into swimming young, which then settle and turn into adults.

LONG LEGS
Spider crabs all have long legs and look like spiders. They hide under rocks and among seaweeds on the lower shore and in shallow waters. Spider crabs make a camouflage by plucking bits of seaweed with their pincers, then attaching these bits to their shells. They crawl over seaweeds hanging on with their claws. Spider crabs can also live on soft sea beds.

Pea crab may nibble mussel's gills

Seaweeds growing on mussel shell

HORSE MUSSEL AND FRIENDS
Heavy-shelled horse mussels live anchored to rocks or kelp holdfasts in shallow water, attached by tough threads. Young mussels settle where another mussel is growing, so gradually a mussel layer builds up on the sea bed. Other creatures live among mussels, but the pea crab takes things a stage further. It makes its home within the shell, feeding on the mussel's food.

Seaweed on legs as part of camouflage

Sharp-tipped claw for hanging onto seaweed

Horse mussel grows to 20 cm (8 in) long

Feathery tentacles held on tough, single stems

Anemone-like polyp with two rings of tentacles to capture food

Sea mat growing on surface

SEA FLOWERS
The beautiful flower-like polyps of this sea fir (hydroid) are used to capture food. If disturbed, the sea fir will withdraw its polyps into its horny skeleton. Sea firs grow fixed to surfaces, such as rocks and seaweeds, putting out branched colonies of anemone-like polyps. Some sea firs reproduce by budding off tiny jellyfish forms, which shed sperm and eggs into the water. The young sea fir then settles on the bottom. This sea fir (right) does not produce such free-floating shapes. Instead, the jellyfish forms stay attached to the parent sea fir which then releases its young.

The coral kingdom

IN THE CRYSTAL CLEAR, WARM WATERS of the tropics, coral reefs flourish, covering vast areas. Made of the skeletons of stony corals, coral reefs are cemented together by chalky algae. Most stony corals are colonies of many tiny, anemone-like individuals, called polyps. Each polyp makes its own hard limestone cup (skeleton) which protects its soft body. To make their skeletons, the coral polyps need the help of microscopic, single-celled algae which live inside them. The algae need sunlight to grow, which is why coral reefs are found only in sunny, surface waters. In return for giving the algae a home, corals get some food from them but also capture plankton with their tentacles. Only the upper layer of a reef is made of living corals, which build upon skeletons of dead polyps. Coral reefs are also home to soft corals and sea fans, which do not have stony skeletons. Related to sea anemones and jellyfish, corals grow in an exquisite variety of shapes (mushroom, daisy, staghorn) and some have colourful skeletons.

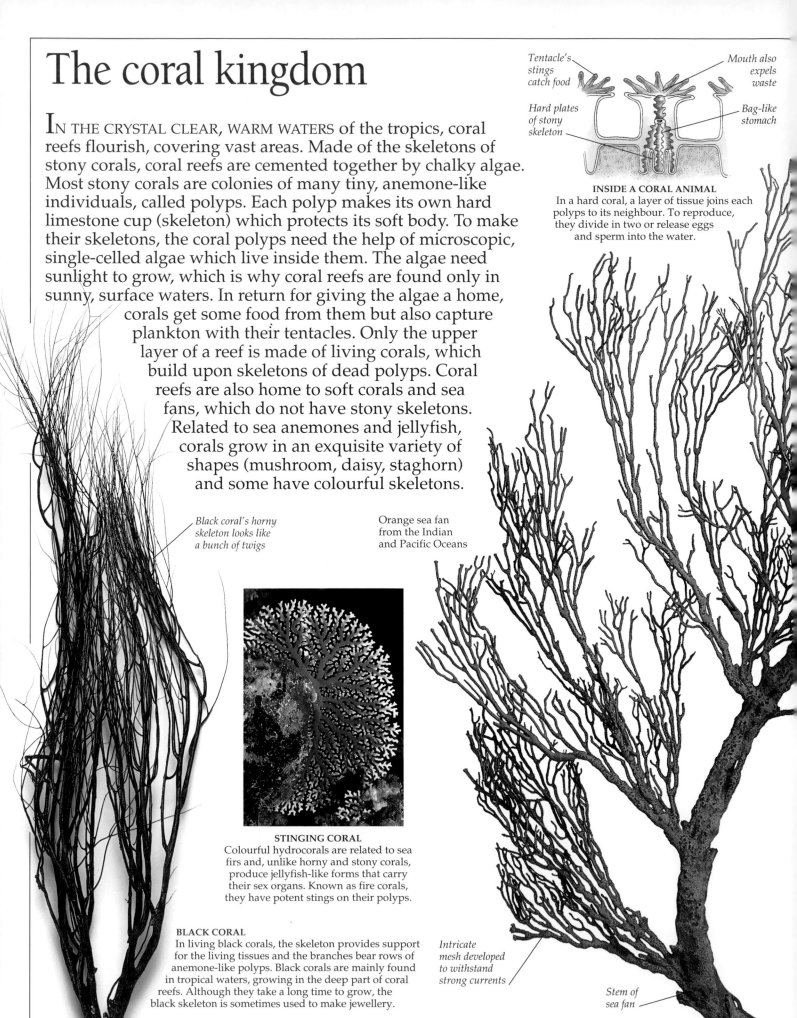

Tentacle's stings catch food

Mouth also expels waste

Hard plates of stony skeleton

Bag-like stomach

INSIDE A CORAL ANIMAL
In a hard coral, a layer of tissue joins each polyps to its neighbour. To reproduce, they divide in two or release eggs and sperm into the water.

Black coral's horny skeleton looks like a bunch of twigs

Orange sea fan from the Indian and Pacific Oceans

STINGING CORAL
Colourful hydrocorals are related to sea firs and, unlike horny and stony corals, produce jellyfish-like forms that carry their sex organs. Known as fire corals, they have potent stings on their polyps.

BLACK CORAL
In living black corals, the skeleton provides support for the living tissues and the branches bear rows of anemone-like polyps. Black corals are mainly found in tropical waters, growing in the deep part of coral reefs. Although they take a long time to grow, the black skeleton is sometimes used to make jewellery.

Intricate mesh developed to withstand strong currents

Stem of sea fan

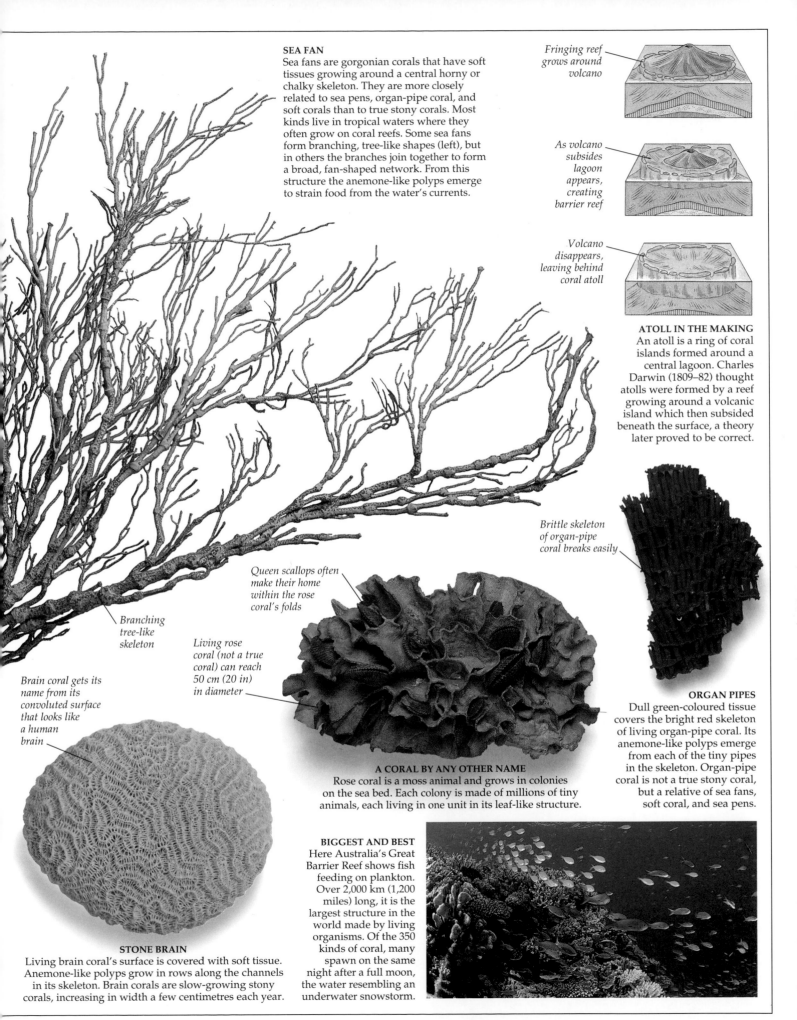

SEA FAN
Sea fans are gorgonian corals that have soft tissues growing around a central horny or chalky skeleton. They are more closely related to sea pens, organ-pipe coral, and soft corals than to true stony corals. Most kinds live in tropical waters where they often grow on coral reefs. Some sea fans form branching, tree-like shapes (left), but in others the branches join together to form a broad, fan-shaped network. From this structure the anemone-like polyps emerge to strain food from the water's currents.

Fringing reef grows around volcano

As volcano subsides lagoon appears, creating barrier reef

Volcano disappears, leaving behind coral atoll

ATOLL IN THE MAKING
An atoll is a ring of coral islands formed around a central lagoon. Charles Darwin (1809–82) thought atolls were formed by a reef growing around a volcanic island which then subsided beneath the surface, a theory later proved to be correct.

Brittle skeleton of organ-pipe coral breaks easily

Branching tree-like skeleton

Queen scallops often make their home within the rose coral's folds

Living rose coral (not a true coral) can reach 50 cm (20 in) in diameter

Brain coral gets its name from its convoluted surface that looks like a human brain

ORGAN PIPES
Dull green-coloured tissue covers the bright red skeleton of living organ-pipe coral. Its anemone-like polyps emerge from each of the tiny pipes in the skeleton. Organ-pipe coral is not a true stony coral, but a relative of sea fans, soft coral, and sea pens.

A CORAL BY ANY OTHER NAME
Rose coral is a moss animal and grows in colonies on the sea bed. Each colony is made of millions of tiny animals, each living in one unit in its leaf-like structure.

BIGGEST AND BEST
Here Australia's Great Barrier Reef shows fish feeding on plankton. Over 2,000 km (1,200 miles) long, it is the largest structure in the world made by living organisms. Of the 350 kinds of coral, many spawn on the same night after a full moon, the water resembling an underwater snowstorm.

STONE BRAIN
Living brain coral's surface is covered with soft tissue. Anemone-like polyps grow in rows along the channels in its skeleton. Brain corals are slow-growing stony corals, increasing in width a few centimetres each year.

Life on a coral reef

A GIANT CLAM

The giant blue clam grows to about 30 cm (1 ft) long, but the largest giant clams may reach 1 m (3 ft 4 in). The colourful mantle exposed at the edge of their shells contains hordes of single-celled algae that make their own food by using the energy from sunlight. The clam gets some food by harvesting this growing crop of algae.

CORAL REEFS HAVE an amazing variety of marine life, from teeming multitudes of brightly coloured fish to giant clams wedged into rocks. Every bit of space on the reef provides a hiding place or shelter for some animal or plant. At night, a host of amazing creatures emerge from coral caves and crevices to feed. All the living organisms on the reef depend for their survival on the stony corals which recycle the scarce nutrients from the clear, blue, tropical waters. People, as well as animals, rely on coral reefs for they protect coastlines, attract tourists' money, and some island nations live on coral atolls. Sadly, in spite of being one of the great natural wonders of the world, coral reefs are now under threat. Destruction is caused by reefs being broken up for building materials, damaged by snorkellers and divers touching or treading on them, dynamited by fishermen, ripped up by curio collectors, covered by soil eroded by the destruction of rain forests, and polluted by sewage and oil spills.

Green colour helps camouflage sea slug amongst seaweeds

Tentacles of sea anemone covered with stings to put off predators

Large eye for keeping a watch for danger

Layer of slimy mucus protects clown fish from anemone's stinging tentacles

Side fin used to steer and change direction

FRILLY LETTUCE
Sea slugs are related to sea snails but do not have shells. Many sea slugs living on coral reefs feed on corals, but the lettuce slug feeds on algae growing on the reef by sucking the sap from individual cells. Chloroplasts, the green part of plant cells, are then stored in the slug's digestive system where they continue to trap energy from sunlight to make food. Many other reef sea slugs are brightly coloured to warn that they are dangerous and recycle the stings that they eat from the coral's tentacles.

Stripes break up clown fish's outline, so it is more difficult for predators to see the fish on the reef

LIVING IN HARMONY
Clown fish which shelter in anemones live on coral reefs in the Pacific and Indian Oceans. Unlike other fish, clown fish are not stung by their anemone home, but protected by a slimy coat of mucus. The anemone's stinging cells are not even triggered by this fish's presence. Clown fish seldom venture far from their anemone home for fear of attack by other fish. There are different kinds of clown fish, some living only with certain kinds of anemones.

DATE MUSSEL
Many different clams live on coral reefs. This date mussel makes its home by producing chemicals to wear a hole in the hard coral. Like most clams, the mussel feeds by collecting food particles from water passing through its gills.

Date mussel on a coral reef in the Red Sea

Narrow snout probes for sponges and other animals that grow on rocks

Bright colours help attract a mate

Plain yellow caudal (tail) fin

Adult emperor angelfish's colours and patterns act as signals to other angelfish

Adult

Special glands in skin make slug taste bad to deter predators

GROWING UP
Angelfish are common inhabitants of coral reefs. The young emperor angelfish looks quite different from the adult possibly because its colours protect it better. Once the adults pair up, they establish a territory on the reef where they can feed. Their colours and patterns help other emperors to recognize them, so they can see their patch of the reef is occupied.

Juvenile

Ring patterns may draw predator away from juvenile's more vulnerable head

Soft body has no shell to protect slug

NOTORIOUS STARFISH
The crown-of-thorns starfish devours the soft parts of a gorgonian coral. Like many others, it feeds by turning its stomach inside out, making enzymes to digest its prey. Plagues of these starfish attacked Australia's Great Barrier Reef in the 1960s and 1970s, killing large numbers of corals, but no one knows why.

Crown-of-thorns starfish eating coral

Flat, slimy foot enables slug to crawl over slippery seaweed

Bright green colour shows slug eats algae

Tentacles can be pulled back inside body for protection

Tentacles around mouth used for feeding

Tough skin

Lettuce slug breathes through its skin, which looks like the leaf of a plant

One of five rows of tube-feet helps sea cucumber crawl

COLOURFUL CUCUMBER
One of the most colourful kinds of sea cucumber lives on or close to reefs in the Indo-Pacific region. Sea cucumbers are echinoderms (pp. 18–19), like starfish, sea urchins, and sea lilies. The sea cucumber puts out its sticky tentacles to feed on small particles of food. Once the food has stuck onto the mucus on the tentacle, it is placed inside the mouth and the food removed.

Special fat tentacles for smelling food

Sea meadows

THE MOST ABUNDANT PLANTS IN THE OCEAN are too small to be seen with the naked eye. Often single-celled, these minute, floating plants are called phytoplankton. Like all plants they need sunlight to grow, so are only found in the ocean's upper zone. With the right conditions, phytoplankton multiply quickly, within a few days, as each cell divides into two, and so on. To grow, phytoplankton need nutrients from the sea water and lots of sunlight. The most light occurs in the tropics but nutrients, especially nitrogen and phosphorus, are in short supply, restricting phytoplankton's growth. Spectacular phytoplankton blooms are found in cooler waters where nutrients (dead plant and animal waste) are brought up from the bottom during storms, and also in both cool and warm waters where there are upwellings of nutrient-rich water. Phytoplankton are eaten by swarms of tiny, drifting animals (zooplankton), which provide a feast for small fish (such as herring), which in turn are eaten by larger fish (such as dogfish), which in their turn are eaten by still larger fish or other predators (such as dolphins). Some larger ocean animals (whale sharks and blue whales) feed directly on zooplankton.

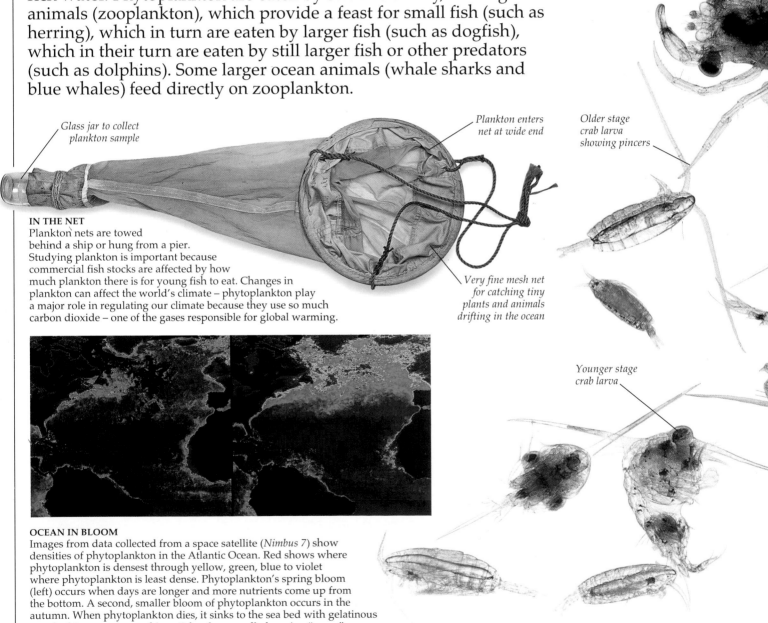

PLANT FOOD
This diatom is one of many phytoplankton that drift in the ocean. Diatoms are the most common kinds of phytoplankton in cooler waters, but dinoflagellates, called single-celled plants, are common in tropical waters. Many diatoms are single cells, but this one consists of a chain of cells.

Glass jar to collect plankton sample

Plankton enters net at wide end

Older stage crab larva showing pincers

IN THE NET
Plankton nets are towed behind a ship or hung from a pier. Studying plankton is important because commercial fish stocks are affected by how much plankton there is for young fish to eat. Changes in plankton can affect the world's climate – phytoplankton play a major role in regulating our climate because they use so much carbon dioxide – one of the gases responsible for global warming.

Very fine mesh net for catching tiny plants and animals drifting in the ocean

Younger stage crab larva

OCEAN IN BLOOM
Images from data collected from a space satellite (*Nimbus 7*) show densities of phytoplankton in the Atlantic Ocean. Red shows where phytoplankton is densest through yellow, green, blue to violet where phytoplankton is least dense. Phytoplankton's spring bloom (left) occurs when days are longer and more nutrients come up from the bottom. A second, smaller bloom of phytoplankton occurs in the autumn. When phytoplankton dies, it sinks to the sea bed with gelatinous zooplankton remains, making sticky clumps called marine "snow".

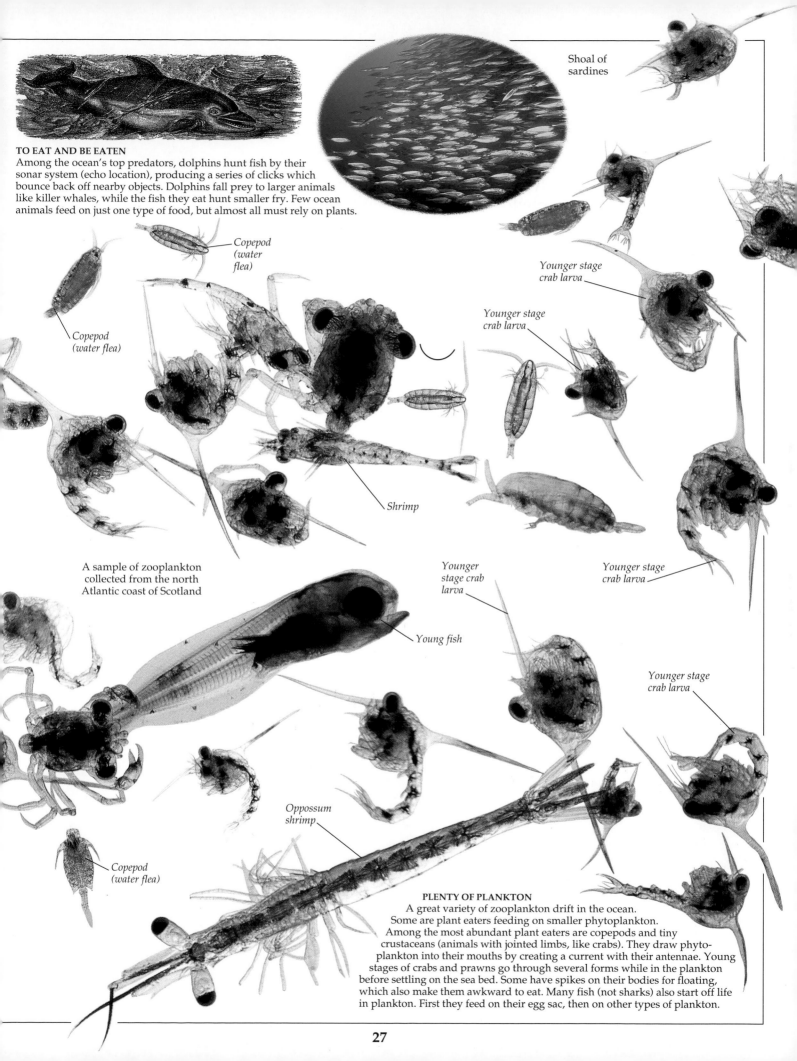

Shoal of sardines

TO EAT AND BE EATEN
Among the ocean's top predators, dolphins hunt fish by their sonar system (echo location), producing a series of clicks which bounce back off nearby objects. Dolphins fall prey to larger animals like killer whales, while the fish they eat hunt smaller fry. Few ocean animals feed on just one type of food, but almost all must rely on plants.

Copepod (water flea)

Copepod (water flea)

Younger stage crab larva

Younger stage crab larva

Shrimp

A sample of zooplankton collected from the north Atlantic coast of Scotland

Younger stage crab larva

Younger stage crab larva

Younger stage crab larva

Younger stage crab larva

Young fish

Oppossum shrimp

Copepod (water flea)

PLENTY OF PLANKTON
A great variety of zooplankton drift in the ocean. Some are plant eaters feeding on smaller phytoplankton. Among the most abundant plant eaters are copepods and tiny crustaceans (animals with jointed limbs, like crabs). They draw phyto-plankton into their mouths by creating a current with their antennae. Young stages of crabs and prawns go through several forms while in the plankton before settling on the sea bed. Some have spikes on their bodies for floating, which also make them awkward to eat. Many fish (not sharks) also start off life in plankton. First they feed on their egg sac, then on other types of plankton.

Predators and prey

SOME OCEAN ANIMALS are herbivores (plant eaters) from certain fish nibbling seaweeds on coral reefs to dugongs chewing seagrasses. There are also many carnivores (meat eaters) in the ocean. Some, such as blue sharks and barracuda, are swift hunters, while others, such as anglerfish and sea anemones, set traps for their prey waiting with snapping jaws or stinging tentacles respectively. Many animals strain food out of the water from the humble sea fan to giant baleen whales. Seabirds also find their meals in the ocean diving for a beakful of prey. Some ocean animals are omnivores – they eat both plants and animals.

CO-OPERATIVE FEEDING
Humpback whales herd shoals of fish by letting out bubbles as they swim around it. Opening their mouths wide to gulp in food and water, they retain fish but expel water through sieve-like baleen plates in their mouths.

Tiny prey caught in mucus

CAUGHT BY SLIME
Unlike many jellyfish which trap prey with their stinging tentacles, common jellyfish catch small drifting animals (plankton) in sticky slime (mucus) produced by the bell. The four fleshy arms beneath the bell collect up the food-laden slime and tiny hair-like cilia channel it into the mouth.

FANG FACE
The wolfish has strong, fang-like teeth for crunching through the hard shells of crabs, sea urchins, and mussels. As the front set are worn down each year, or broken, they are replaced by a new set which grow in behind the old teeth. Wolfish live in cool, deep, northern waters where they lurk in rocky holes.

Dorsal fin runs along entire length of body

Crooked, yellow fang-like teeth

Pectoral fin

Tough, wrinkled skin helps protect wolfish living near the sea bed

28

Spines to protect urchin

GRAZING AWAY

The European common sea urchin grazes on seaweeds and animals such as sea mats that grow on the surface of seaweeds. The urchin uses the rasping teeth on the underside of its shell, that are operated by a complex set of jaws inside, known as Aristotle's lantern. The grazing activities of urchins can control how much seaweed grows in an area, so if too many urchins are collected for food or tourist souvenirs, a rocky reef can become overgrown by seaweed.

Pelican diving

Brown pelican catches fish in pouch-like beak

Tube-feet used to walk slowly along the sea bed

Sea urchin's mouth surrounded by five rasping teeth

Tiny teeth of a basking shark

FEEDING ON FISHES

Like all pelicans, the brown pelican has a big beak with a large flap of skin or pouch to capture a variety of fish. Once they have spotted their prey, they dive into the water, but are too bulky to dive too far below the surface. Only brown pelicans dive for their prey. When the pelican surfaces, water is drained from the pouch and the fish swallowed.

TO BITE OR NOT TO BITE

A tiger shark's tooth is like a multi-purpose tool with a sharp point for piercing prey and a serrated blade-like edge for slicing. This shark can eat almost anything from hard-shelled turtles to soft-bodied seals and seabirds. The rows of a basking shark's tiny teeth are not used at all, since this shark filters food out of the water with a sieve of gill rakers.

Stinging tentacle

TENTACLE TRAPS

The flower-like Dahlia anemones are deadly traps for unwary prawns and small fish that stray too close to their stinging tentacles. When the prey brush past, hundreds of nematocysts (stinging cells) are triggered and fire their stings. So these stings ensnare and weaken the prey. The tentacles pass the stricken prey towards the mouth in the anemone's centre – the entrance to the bag-like stomach where the prey is digested.

Tiger shark's tooth

Any undigested pieces of food are ejected through the mouth

Sucker-like disc lets Dahlia anemone attach to any hard surface

Homes and hiding

STAYING HIDDEN is one of the best means of defence – if a predator cannot see you, it cannot eat you! Many sea animals shelter among seaweeds, in rocky crevices, or under the sand. Matching the colours and even the texture of the background also helps sea creatures remain undetected. The sargassum fish even look like bits of seaweed. Hard shells are useful armour, at least giving protection from weak-jawed predators. Sea snails and clams make their own shells which cover the body. Crab and lobsters have outer shells, like suits of armour, covering the body and each jointed limb. The hermit crab is unusual because only the front part of the body and the legs are covered by a hard shell. Its abdomen is soft, so a hermit crab uses the empty shell of a sea snail to protect itself.

WHAT A WEED
This fish lives among floating clumps of sargassum seaweed, where frilly growths on its head, body, and fins help it avoid being seen by predators, making a realistic disguise. Many different animals live in sargassum seaweed, which drifts in large quantities in the Sargasso Sea of the North Atlantic.

BLENDING IN
Cuttlefish have different coloured pigments and rapidly change colour to escape predators. Their eyes perceive their surroundings and nerve signals are sent by the brain to tiny bags of pigment in the skin. When these pigment bags contract, the cuttlefish's colour becomes lighter.

Cuttlefish becomes darker when pigment bags expand

Hermit crab leaving old whelk shell

Anemone

Investigating its new home by checking size with its claws

When out of its shell, crab is vulnerable to predators

Leg with pointed claws to get a grip on sea bed when walking

Antenna

ALL CHANGE
Like all crustaceans, a hermit crab grows by shedding its hard, outer skeleton and does this within the safety of its snail shell home. As it grows larger, it needs to find a larger snail shell to move into. Before leaving its old shell, it will test the size of a new home. If it is not large enough or is cracked, the hermit crab looks for another shell. When the hermit crab has found one which is just right, it carefully pulls its body out of its old shell, tucking it quickly into the new shell. As the hermit crab grows larger it moves into large whelk shells and lives in shallow water submerged on the sea bed.

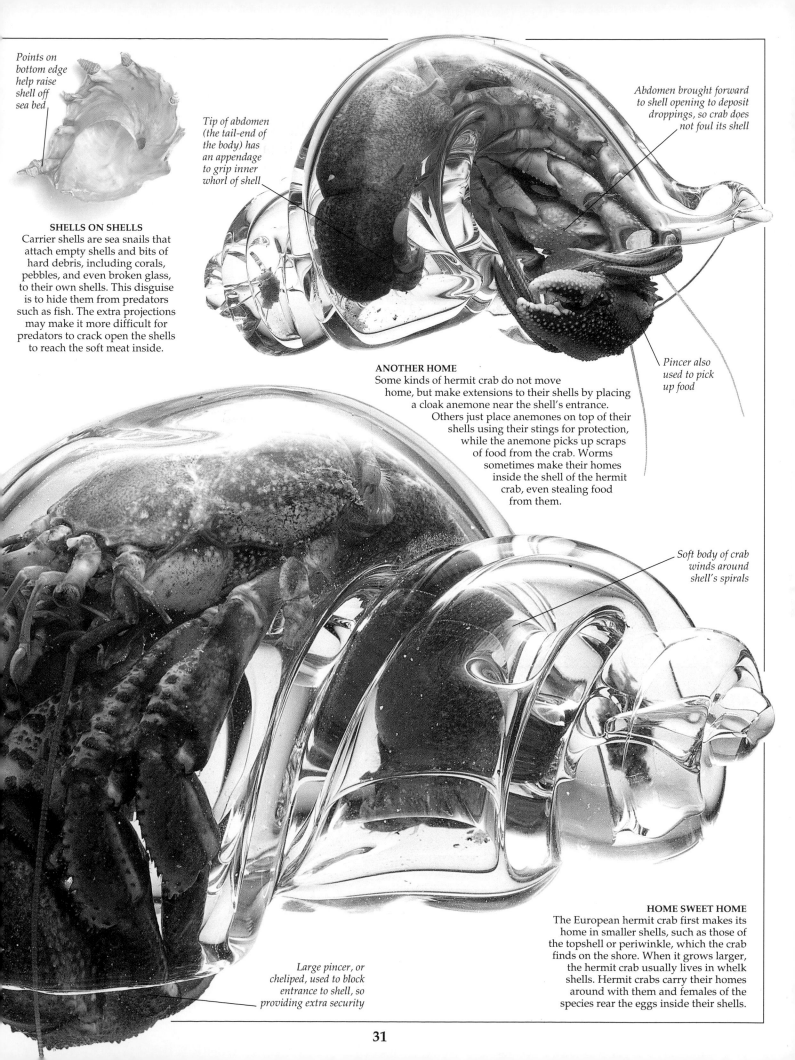

Points on bottom edge help raise shell off sea bed

Tip of abdomen (the tail-end of the body) has an appendage to grip inner whorl of shell

Abdomen brought forward to shell opening to deposit droppings, so crab does not foul its shell

SHELLS ON SHELLS

Carrier shells are sea snails that attach empty shells and bits of hard debris, including corals, pebbles, and even broken glass, to their own shells. This disguise is to hide them from predators such as fish. The extra projections may make it more difficult for predators to crack open the shells to reach the soft meat inside.

Pincer also used to pick up food

ANOTHER HOME

Some kinds of hermit crab do not move home, but make extensions to their shells by placing a cloak anemone near the shell's entrance. Others just place anemones on top of their shells using their stings for protection, while the anemone picks up scraps of food from the crab. Worms sometimes make their homes inside the shell of the hermit crab, even stealing food from them.

Soft body of crab winds around shell's spirals

Large pincer, or cheliped, used to block entrance to shell, so providing extra security

HOME SWEET HOME

The European hermit crab first makes its home in smaller shells, such as those of the topshell or periwinkle, which the crab finds on the shore. When it grows larger, the hermit crab usually lives in whelk shells. Hermit crabs carry their homes around with them and females of the species rear the eggs inside their shells.

Attack and defence

Many sea creatures have weapons to defend themselves from predators or to attack prey. Some produce venom (poison) for defence and often advertise their danger with distinctive markings. Lionfish's stripes alert their enemies that they are armed with venomous spines but being easy to see, they have to surprise their prey as they hunt in the open or ambush them from behind clumps of coral. Stonefish are armed with venomous spines too, opting to blend perfectly with their background when waiting on a reef for prey to swim by. Octopi change colour to that of their background. If attacked the blue-ringed octopus produces blue spots to warn that its bite is poisonous. Disappearing in a cloud of ink is another useful trick used by octopi, squid, and cuttlefish. Most clams can withdraw their delicate soft parts into their shells, but the gaping file shell's tentacles are a deterrent producing an irritating sticky fluid. But no defence method is foolproof. Even the most venomous jellyfish can be eaten by carnivorous turtles that are immune to their stings.

DEADLY STONEFISH
The stonefish is one of the most deadly creatures in the ocean. A stonefish's venom, which is injected through the sharp spines on its back, causes such intense pain that a person treading on one may go into shock and die.

Ink cloud forming around cuttlefish

Long, dorsal spine with venom glands in grooves

INK SCREEN
Cephalopods, which include cuttlefish, squid, and octopi, produce a cloud of ink when threatened, to confuse an enemy and allow time for escape. The ink, produced in a gland linked to the gut, is ejected in a blast of water from a tube-like funnel near its head.

Horny projection above eye

Maerl (a chalky, red seaweed) grows in a thick mass along the stony sea bed

Three venomous anal spines

KEEP CLEAR
The striped body of lionfish warn predators that they are dangerous. A predator trying to bite a lionfish may be impaled by one or more of its poisonous spines. If it survives, the predator will remember the danger and leave the lionfish alone in future. Lionfish can swim openly looking for smaller prey with little risk of attack. They live in tropical waters from the Indian to the Pacific Oceans. In spite of being poisonous, they are popular aquarium fish because of their beauty.

Stripes warn predators that lionfish is dangerous

BLUE FOR DANGER
If this octopus becomes irritated, or when it is feeding, blue-ringed spots appear on its skin, warning of its poisonous bite. Although this octopus is similar in size to a person's hand, its bite can sometimes be fatal. Blue-ringed octopi live in shallow waters around Australia and some Pacific Ocean islands.

Two venomous spines on tail can pierce the swimmer's skin and inject its venom

Painting of sea monsters, c. 1880s

Sting ray's sting is sharp and serrated so it can easily pierce the skin

Pectoral fin used for swimming

STING IN THE TAIL
This blue-spotted ray lives in the warm waters of both the Indian and Pacific Oceans as well as the Red Sea, where it is often found lurking on the sandy sea bed. If trodden on, shooting pains occur in the foot for over an hour, but after six, the pain gradually wears off.

SOMETHING SCARY
Early sailors knew that some creatures living in the sea were dangerous and could kill people. Tales about these sea monsters, though common, often became greatly exaggerated. Monster stories were also invented to account for ships which foundered due to dangerous sea conditions.

VICIOUS JELLYFISH
Jellyfish are well-known for their nasty stings, but the nastiest are those of the box jellyfish, which swim near the coasts of northern Australia and southeast Asia. Its stings produce horrible welts on anyone who comes in contact with their tentacles. A badly stung person can die in four minutes.

When shell is closed, there is still a gap between the shell's two halves

Tentacles always on show

SHAGGY SHELLS
These gaping file shells cannot withdraw their masses of orange tentacles inside the two halves of their shell for protection, so the tentacles produce a sour-tasting, sticky substance to deter predators. If tentacles are nibbled off, they can regrow. Gaping file shells build homes in seaweed, by putting out byssus threads for anchorage. They can also make "nests" among horse mussels and oarweeds. If dislodged from their homes, they can move by expelling water from their shell and using their tentacles like oars.

Shell is up to 2.54 cm (1 in) long

The jet set

ONE WAY TO GET AROUND QUICKLY in water is by jet propulsion. Some molluscs, such as clams, squid, and octopi, do this by squirting water from the body cavity. Jet propulsion can be used both for swimming and to help molluscs escape from predators. Squid are best at jet propulsion – their bodies are permanently streamlined to reduce drag (resistance to water). Some kinds of scallops also use jet propulsion and are among the few clams that can swim. Most clams (molluscs with shells in two halves) can only bury themselves in the sand, or are anchored to the sea bed. The common octopus lives on the rocky sea bed in the coastal waters of the Atlantic Ocean, and the Mediterranean and Caribbean Seas. If attacked, it can jet off.

TENTACLE TALES
A Norwegian story tells of the Kraken, a giant sea monster that wrapped its arms around ships before sinking them. The legend may be based on the mysterious giant squid which live in deep waters. Dead individuals sometimes are seen washed up on the shore, but no one has ever seen them swimming in the depths.

JET PROPULSION
The engines powering jet planes produce jets of air to fly in much the same way that octopi, squid, and cuttlefish produce jets of water to propel themselves through the water.

Funnel

FLEXIBLE FUNNEL
Sticking out from the edge of the octopus's bag-like body is its funnel. The funnel can be bent so the jet of water can be aimed backwards or forwards, to control the direction in which the octopus heads off.

Long arms to grasp prey

Powerful suckers grip the rock, so octopus can pull itself along

1 ON THE BOTTOM
The common octopus hides during the day in its rocky lair, coming out at night to look for such food as crustaceans. The octopus slowly approaches its prey, then pounces, wrapping it between the webbing at the base of its arms.

Sucker is sensitive to touch and taste

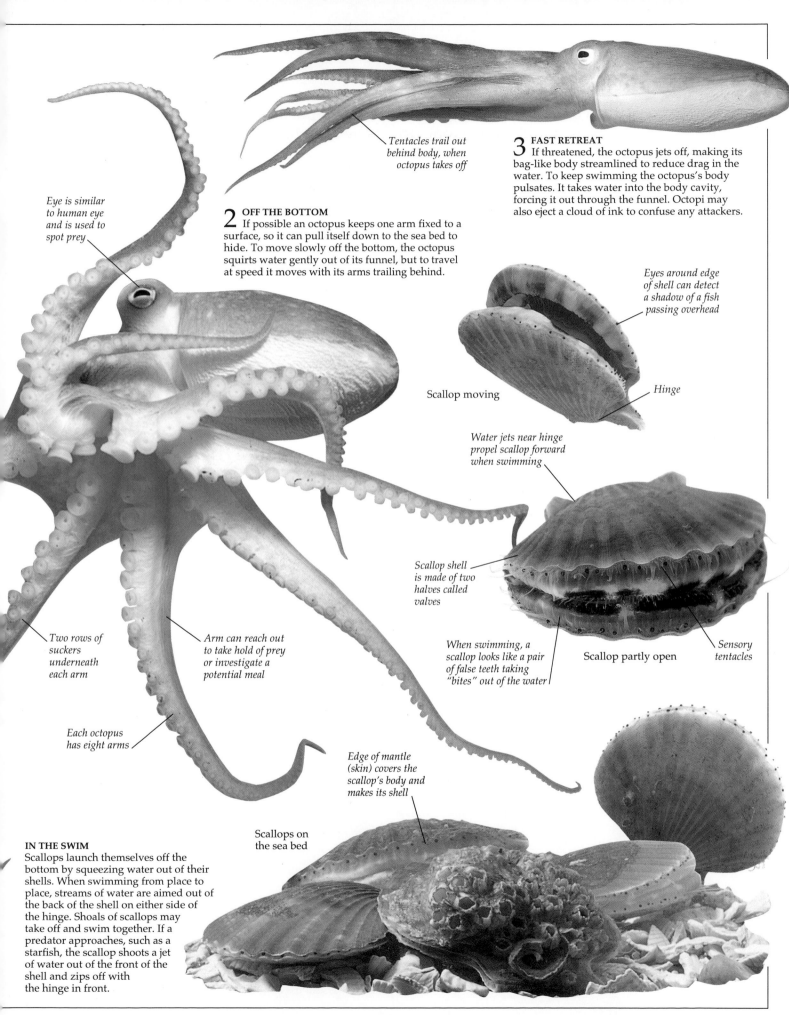

Tentacles trail out behind body, when octopus takes off

Eye is similar to human eye and is used to spot prey

2 OFF THE BOTTOM
If possible an octopus keeps one arm fixed to a surface, so it can pull itself down to the sea bed to hide. To move slowly off the bottom, the octopus squirts water gently out of its funnel, but to travel at speed it moves with its arms trailing behind.

3 FAST RETREAT
If threatened, the octopus jets off, making its bag-like body streamlined to reduce drag in the water. To keep swimming the octopus's body pulsates. It takes water into the body cavity, forcing it out through the funnel. Octopi may also eject a cloud of ink to confuse any attackers.

Eyes around edge of shell can detect a shadow of a fish passing overhead

Scallop moving

Hinge

Water jets near hinge propel scallop forward when swimming

Scallop shell is made of two halves called valves

Two rows of suckers underneath each arm

Arm can reach out to take hold of prey or investigate a potential meal

When swimming, a scallop looks like a pair of false teeth taking "bites" out of the water

Scallop partly open

Sensory tentacles

Each octopus has eight arms

Edge of mantle (skin) covers the scallop's body and makes its shell

IN THE SWIM
Scallops launch themselves off the bottom by squeezing water out of their shells. When swimming from place to place, streams of water are aimed out of the back of the shell on either side of the hinge. Shoals of scallops may take off and swim together. If a predator approaches, such as a starfish, the scallop shoots a jet of water out of the front of the shell and zips off with the hinge in front.

Scallops on the sea bed

35

Moving along

FLYING FISH
Gathering speed underwater, flying fish leap clear of the surface to escape predators, then glide for more than 30 seconds by spreading out the side fins.

AT SCHOOL
Fish often swim together in a shoal or school (like these blue-striped snappers), where a single fish has less chance of being attacked by a predator than when swimming on its own. The moving mass of individuals may confuse a predator and also there are more pairs of eyes on the look-out for an attacker.

Every swimmer knows that it is harder to move an arm or a leg through seawater than through air. This is because seawater is much denser than air. To be a fast swimmer like a dolphin, tuna, or sailfish, it helps to have a shape which is streamlined like a torpedo to reduce drag (resistance to water). A smooth skin and few projections from the body allow an animal to move through the water more easily. The density of seawater does have an advantage, in that it helps to support the weight of an animal's body. The heaviest animal that ever lived on earth is the blue whale, which weighs up to 150 tonnes (147.6 tons). Some heavy-shelled creatures, like the chambered nautilus, have gas-filled floats to stop them from sinking. Some ocean animals, such as dolphins and flying fish, get up enough speed underwater to leap briefly into the air, but not all ocean animals are good swimmers. Many can only swim slowly, some drift along in the currents, crawl along the bottom, burrow in the sand, or stay put, anchored to the sea bed.

IN THE SWING
During the day, many electric rays prefer to stay hidden on the sandy bottom, as well as relying on their electric organs for defence, but they do swim if disturbed and at night when searching for prey. There are over 30 different kinds of electric ray, mostly living in warm waters. Most other rays have spindly tails (unlike the electric ray's broad tail), so move through water using their pectoral fins. Waves pass from the front to the back of the pectoral fins which, in larger rays such as mantas, become so exaggerated that the fins actually beat up and down.

Electric ray's smooth skin can be either blackish or red-brown in colour

Spiracle (a one-way valve) takes in water which is pumped out through gill slits underneath

Some electric rays can grow to 1.8 m (6 ft) and weigh as much as 50 kg (110 lb)

Swimming sequence of an electric ray

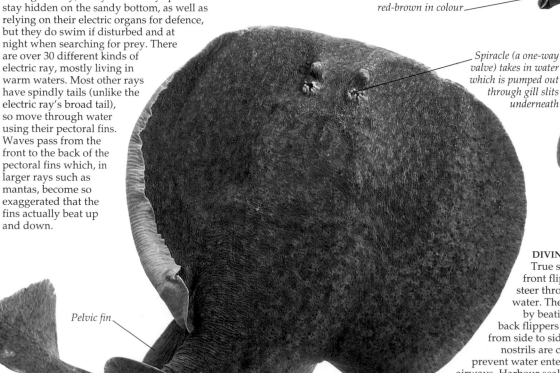

Pelvic fin

DIVING DEEP
True seals use front flippers to steer through the water. They move by beating their back flippers and tail from side to side. Their nostrils are closed to prevent water entering the airways. Harbour seals (right) can dive to 90 m (300 ft), but the champion seal diver is the Antarctic's Weddell seal, diving to 600 m (2,000 ft). Seals do not get the bends, because they breathe out before diving and, unlike humans, do not breathe compressed air. When underwater, seals use oxygen stored in the blood.

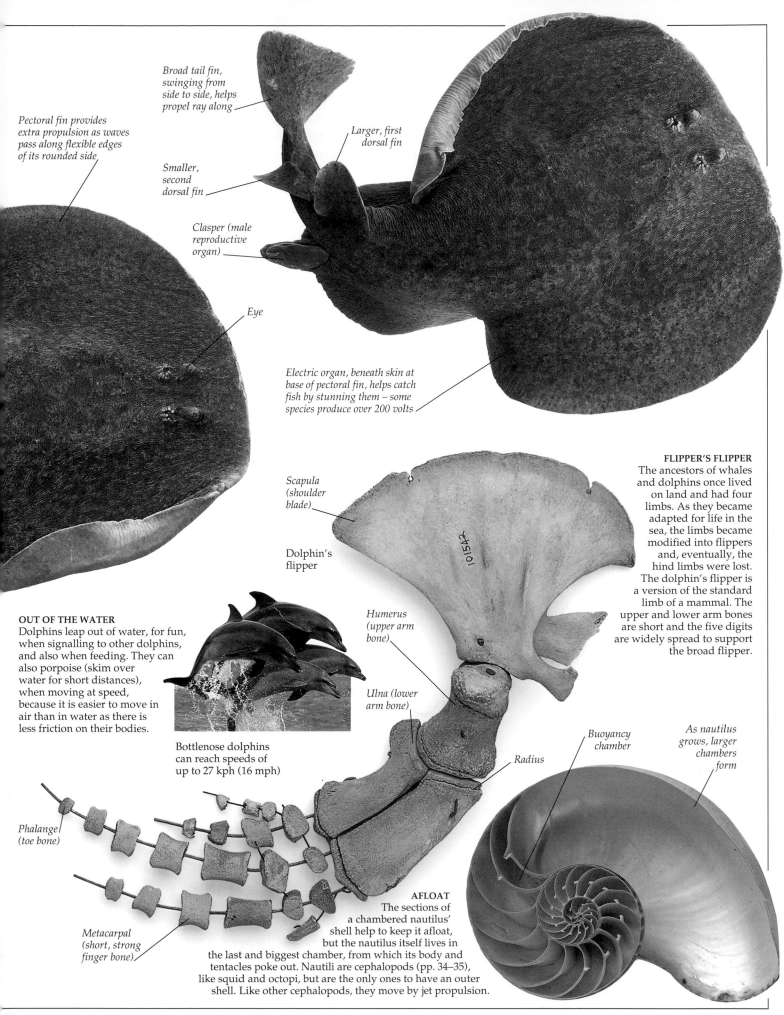

Broad tail fin, swinging from side to side, helps propel ray along

Pectoral fin provides extra propulsion as waves pass along flexible edges of its rounded side

Larger, first dorsal fin

Smaller, second dorsal fin

Clasper (male reproductive organ)

Eye

Electric organ, beneath skin at base of pectoral fin, helps catch fish by stunning them – some species produce over 200 volts

Scapula (shoulder blade)

Dolphin's flipper

FLIPPER'S FLIPPER
The ancestors of whales and dolphins once lived on land and had four limbs. As they became adapted for life in the sea, the limbs became modified into flippers and, eventually, the hind limbs were lost. The dolphin's flipper is a version of the standard limb of a mammal. The upper and lower arm bones are short and the five digits are widely spread to support the broad flipper.

OUT OF THE WATER
Dolphins leap out of water, for fun, when signalling to other dolphins, and also when feeding. They can also porpoise (skim over water for short distances), when moving at speed, because it is easier to move in air than in water as there is less friction on their bodies.

Bottlenose dolphins can reach speeds of up to 27 kph (16 mph)

Humerus (upper arm bone)

Ulna (lower arm bone)

Radius

Buoyancy chamber

As nautilus grows, larger chambers form

Phalange (toe bone)

Metacarpal (short, strong finger bone)

AFLOAT
The sections of a chambered nautilus' shell help to keep it afloat, but the nautilus itself lives in the last and biggest chamber, from which its body and tentacles poke out. Nautili are cephalopods (pp. 34–35), like squid and octopi, but are the only ones to have an outer shell. Like other cephalopods, they move by jet propulsion.

Ocean travellers

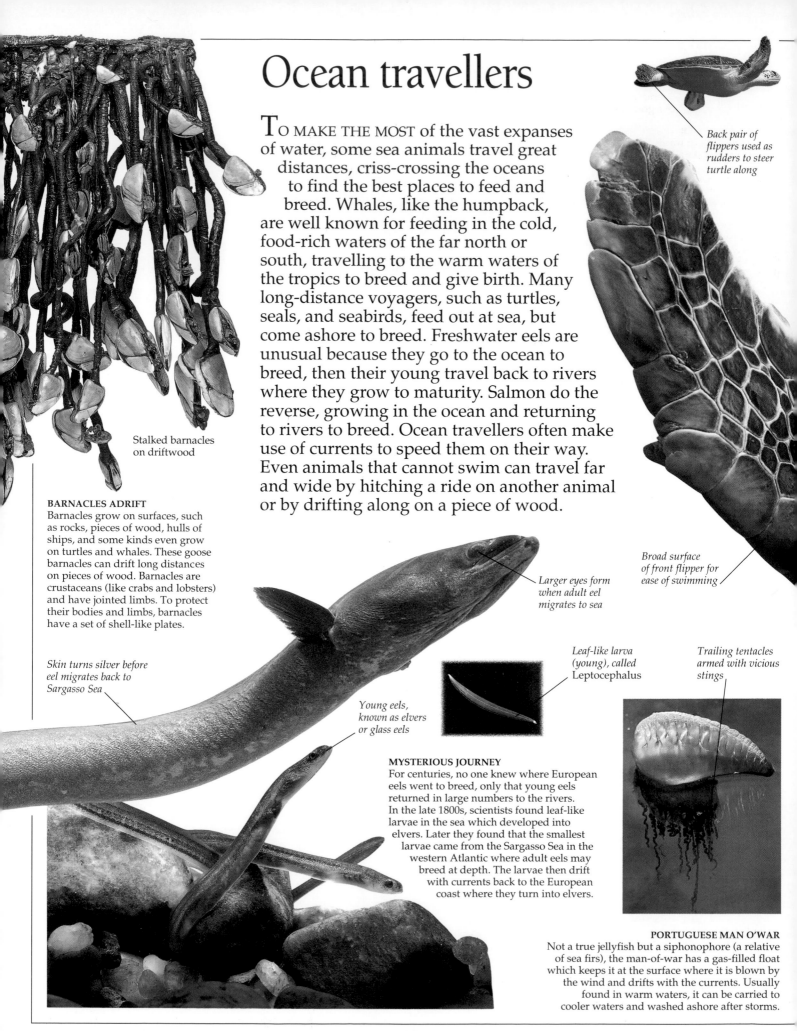

To make the most of the vast expanses of water, some sea animals travel great distances, criss-crossing the oceans to find the best places to feed and breed. Whales, like the humpback, are well known for feeding in the cold, food-rich waters of the far north or south, travelling to the warm waters of the tropics to breed and give birth. Many long-distance voyagers, such as turtles, seals, and seabirds, feed out at sea, but come ashore to breed. Freshwater eels are unusual because they go to the ocean to breed, then their young travel back to rivers where they grow to maturity. Salmon do the reverse, growing in the ocean and returning to rivers to breed. Ocean travellers often make use of currents to speed them on their way. Even animals that cannot swim can travel far and wide by hitching a ride on another animal or by drifting along on a piece of wood.

Back pair of flippers used as rudders to steer turtle along

Stalked barnacles on driftwood

BARNACLES ADRIFT
Barnacles grow on surfaces, such as rocks, pieces of wood, hulls of ships, and some kinds even grow on turtles and whales. These goose barnacles can drift long distances on pieces of wood. Barnacles are crustaceans (like crabs and lobsters) and have jointed limbs. To protect their bodies and limbs, barnacles have a set of shell-like plates.

Broad surface of front flipper for ease of swimming

Larger eyes form when adult eel migrates to sea

Skin turns silver before eel migrates back to Sargasso Sea

Leaf-like larva (young), called Leptocephalus

Trailing tentacles armed with vicious stings

Young eels, known as elvers or glass eels

MYSTERIOUS JOURNEY
For centuries, no one knew where European eels went to breed, only that young eels returned in large numbers to the rivers. In the late 1800s, scientists found leaf-like larvae in the sea which developed into elvers. Later they found that the smallest larvae came from the Sargasso Sea in the western Atlantic where adult eels may breed at depth. The larvae then drift with currents back to the European coast where they turn into elvers.

PORTUGUESE MAN O'WAR
Not a true jellyfish but a siphonophore (a relative of sea firs), the man-of-war has a gas-filled float which keeps it at the surface where it is blown by the wind and drifts with the currents. Usually found in warm waters, it can be carried to cooler waters and washed ashore after storms.

Swimming sequence
of a green turtle

*Turtle shell is
streamlined for
gliding through
water*

UNDERWATER FLIER

Green turtles live in warm waters in the Atlantic, Pacific, and
Indian Oceans. Like all turtles, they come ashore to lay their
eggs. First the females mate in shallow water with the waiting
males. Later, under cover of darkness, the females crawl up
the beach to lay their eggs in the sand before heading
back to the water. They may return several times
in one breeding season to lay further batches
of eggs. Some green turtles are known
to travel several hundred kilometres
or more to reach their breeding
beaches where they hatched
themselves. Green turtles
feed on sea grasses
and seaweeds.

*Front pair of
flippers help
turtle to "fly"
through water*

*Turtles are
air breathers,
so must come
to surface to
breathe
through their
nostrils*

Green turtle
(*Chelonia mydas*)
is on the
endangered
species list

TURTLE TRIP

In the Japanese legend, Urashima Taro rides into the
kingdom of the sea on a turtle. After spending some time in
the depths, he begs the sea goddess to let him go home. She
allows this, but gives him a box which he must never open.
On his return he finds his home has changed and no one
knows him. Hoping for some comfort, he opens the box·but
the spell is broken. He becomes a very old man because
he has spent not three years – but 300 – in the sea.

The twilight zone

Between the bright sunlit waters of the upper ocean and the pitch black depths is the half-light of the twilight zone which ranges from 200 to 1000 m (660 to 3300 ft) below the surface. Fish living in the twilight zone often have rows of light organs on their undersides to help camouflage them against the little light filtering down from above. These glowing lights can be produced by chemical reactions or by colonies of bacteria living in the light organs. Many animals, including some lantern fish and a variety of squid, only spend their days in the twilight zone. At night they journey upwards to feed in the food-rich surface water. By doing this, they are less at risk from daytime hunters such as seabirds. Others, such as the lancet fish, spend their lives in the twilight zone eating any available food. The skinny lancet fish has a stretchy stomach so it takes a large meal if it finds one.

HUNTER OF THE DEPTHS
Viper fish have an impressive set of dagger-like teeth to grab their fish prey, which they attract with a lure dangling from the front of the dorsal fin. The extra-long teeth in the bottom jaw are too large to fit inside the mouth when the jaws are closed. When swallowing prey, such as a hatchet fish (above left), the hinged jaws open very wide.

Jumbo squid can reach 3.6 m (12 ft) to the tips of their tentacles

A GIANT OF A SQUID
Any squid over 0.5 m (20 in) long can be named a giant squid – the largest can weigh one tonne. Suckers line the arms and tentacles to cling onto prey. Sperm whales often bear sucker-shaped scars where they have grappled with squid.

Fin ray

Sail-like dorsal fin can be raised and lowered

Dorsal fin can be used for herding fish prey

MERMAN
Many strange creatures lurk in the ocean depths, but no one is likely to find one looking like this.

Large gill flap

Model of a lancet fish

Pointed teeth for grabbing fish

Pectoral fin

LONG AND SKINNY
The lancet fish only weighs a couple of kilos (4.5 lb), because it has a narrow body, lightweight bones, and not much muscle. A predator, it catches squid and other fish, such as hatchet fish, living at the same depths.

Pelvic fin

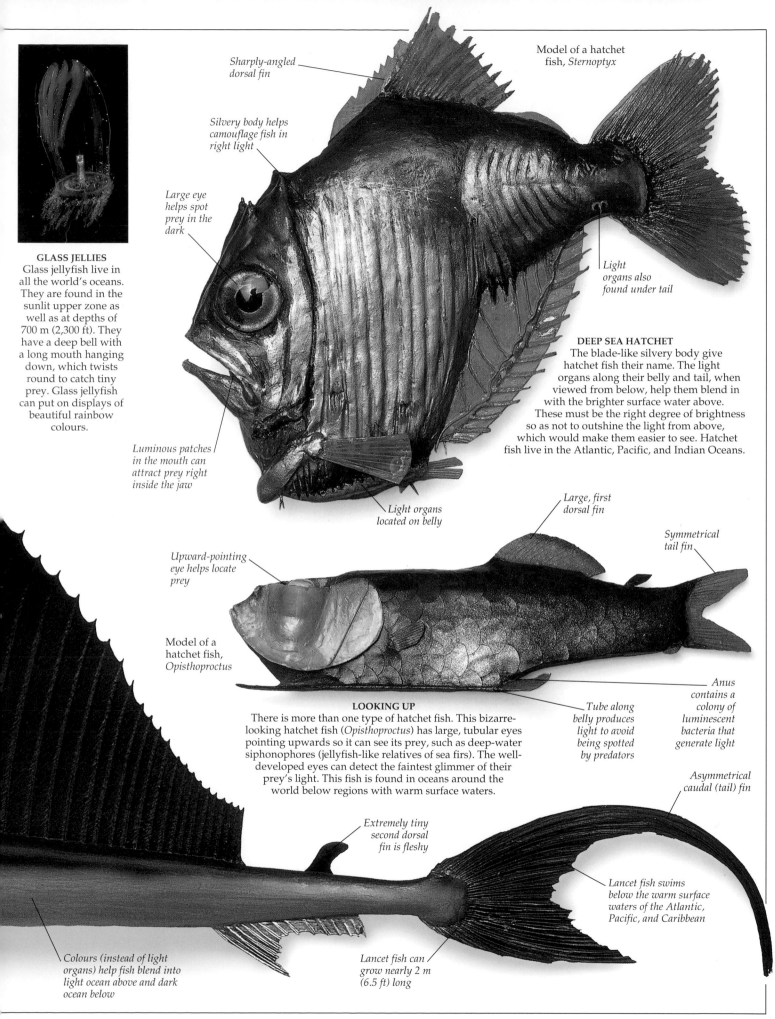

Model of a hatchet
fish, *Sternoptyx*

*Sharply-angled
dorsal fin*

*Silvery body helps
camouflage fish in
right light*

*Large eye
helps spot
prey in the
dark*

*Light
organs also
found under tail*

DEEP SEA HATCHET
The blade-like silvery body give
hatchet fish their name. The light
organs along their belly and tail, when
viewed from below, help them blend in
with the brighter surface water above.
These must be the right degree of brightness
so as not to outshine the light from above,
which would make them easier to see. Hatchet
fish live in the Atlantic, Pacific, and Indian Oceans.

GLASS JELLIES
Glass jellyfish live in
all the world's oceans.
They are found in the
sunlit upper zone as
well as at depths of
700 m (2,300 ft). They
have a deep bell with
a long mouth hanging
down, which twists
round to catch tiny
prey. Glass jellyfish
can put on displays of
beautiful rainbow
colours.

*Luminous patches
in the mouth can
attract prey right
inside the jaw*

*Light organs
located on belly*

*Upward-pointing
eye helps locate
prey*

Model of a
hatchet fish,
Opisthoproctus

LOOKING UP
There is more than one type of hatchet fish. This bizarre-
looking hatchet fish (*Opisthoproctus*) has large, tubular eyes
pointing upwards so it can see its prey, such as deep-water
siphonophores (jellyfish-like relatives of sea firs). The well-
developed eyes can detect the faintest glimmer of their
prey's light. This fish is found in oceans around the
world below regions with warm surface waters.

*Large, first
dorsal fin*

*Symmetrical
tail fin*

*Anus
contains a
colony of
luminescent
bacteria that
generate light*

*Tube along
belly produces
light to avoid
being spotted
by predators*

*Asymmetrical
caudal (tail) fin*

*Extremely tiny
second dorsal
fin is fleshy*

*Lancet fish swims
below the warm surface
waters of the Atlantic,
Pacific, and Caribbean*

*Colours (instead of light
organs) help fish blend into
light ocean above and dark
ocean below*

*Lancet fish can
grow nearly 2 m
(6.5 ft) long*

The darkest depths

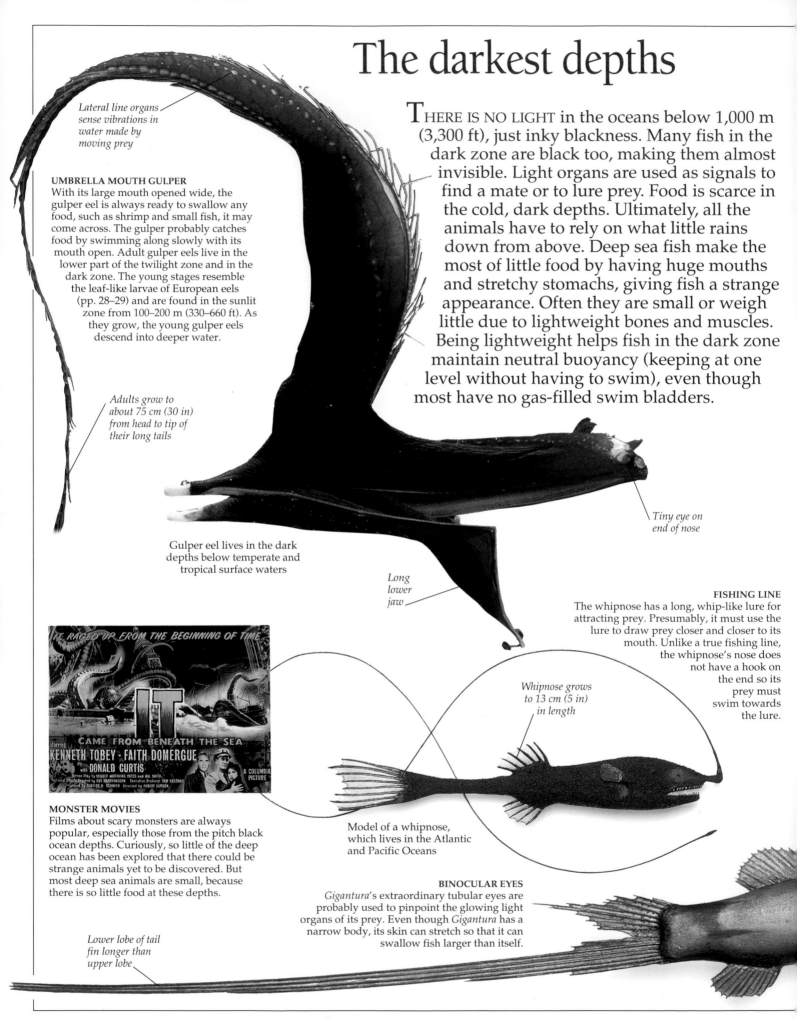

THERE IS NO LIGHT in the oceans below 1,000 m (3,300 ft), just inky blackness. Many fish in the dark zone are black too, making them almost invisible. Light organs are used as signals to find a mate or to lure prey. Food is scarce in the cold, dark depths. Ultimately, all the animals have to rely on what little rains down from above. Deep sea fish make the most of little food by having huge mouths and stretchy stomachs, giving fish a strange appearance. Often they are small or weigh little due to lightweight bones and muscles. Being lightweight helps fish in the dark zone maintain neutral buoyancy (keeping at one level without having to swim), even though most have no gas-filled swim bladders.

Lateral line organs sense vibrations in water made by moving prey

UMBRELLA MOUTH GULPER
With its large mouth opened wide, the gulper eel is always ready to swallow any food, such as shrimp and small fish, it may come across. The gulper probably catches food by swimming along slowly with its mouth open. Adult gulper eels live in the lower part of the twilight zone and in the dark zone. The young stages resemble the leaf-like larvae of European eels (pp. 28–29) and are found in the sunlit zone from 100–200 m (330–660 ft). As they grow, the young gulper eels descend into deeper water.

Adults grow to about 75 cm (30 in) from head to tip of their long tails

Gulper eel lives in the dark depths below temperate and tropical surface waters

Tiny eye on end of nose

Long lower jaw

FISHING LINE
The whipnose has a long, whip-like lure for attracting prey. Presumably, it must use the lure to draw prey closer and closer to its mouth. Unlike a true fishing line, the whipnose's nose does not have a hook on the end so its prey must swim towards the lure.

Whipnose grows to 13 cm (5 in) in length

IT RAGED UP FROM THE BEGINNING OF TIME
IT
starring
CAME FROM BENEATH THE SEA
KENNETH TOBEY · FAITH DOMERGUE
with DONALD CURTIS
A COLUMBIA PICTURE

MONSTER MOVIES
Films about scary monsters are always popular, especially those from the pitch black ocean depths. Curiously, so little of the deep ocean has been explored that there could be strange animals yet to be discovered. But most deep sea animals are small, because there is so little food at these depths.

Model of a whipnose, which lives in the Atlantic and Pacific Oceans

BINOCULAR EYES
Gigantura's extraordinary tubular eyes are probably used to pinpoint the glowing light organs of its prey. Even though *Gigantura* has a narrow body, its skin can stretch so that it can swallow fish larger than itself.

Lower lobe of tail fin longer than upper lobe

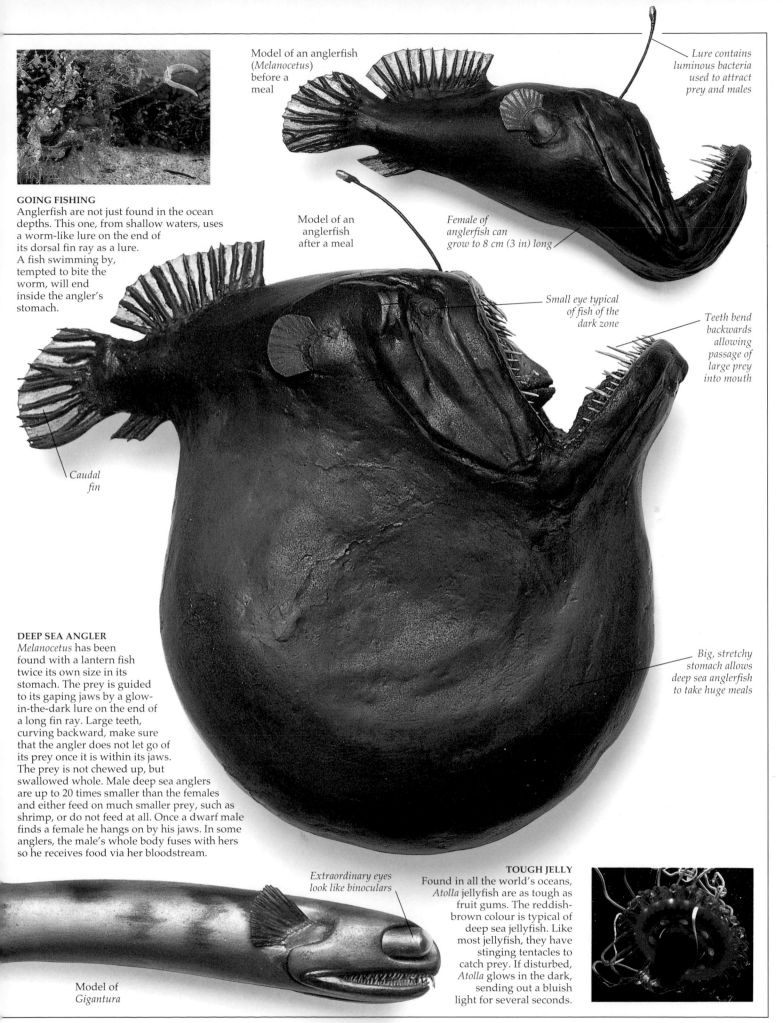

Model of an anglerfish (*Melanocetus*) before a meal

Lure contains luminous bacteria used to attract prey and males

Model of an anglerfish after a meal

Female of anglerfish can grow to 8 cm (3 in) long

Small eye typical of fish of the dark zone

Teeth bend backwards allowing passage of large prey into mouth

GOING FISHING

Anglerfish are not just found in the ocean depths. This one, from shallow waters, uses a worm-like lure on the end of its dorsal fin ray as a lure. A fish swimming by, tempted to bite the worm, will end inside the angler's stomach.

Caudal fin

DEEP SEA ANGLER

Melanocetus has been found with a lantern fish twice its own size in its stomach. The prey is guided to its gaping jaws by a glow-in-the-dark lure on the end of a long fin ray. Large teeth, curving backward, make sure that the angler does not let go of its prey once it is within its jaws. The prey is not chewed up, but swallowed whole. Male deep sea anglers are up to 20 times smaller than the females and either feed on much smaller prey, such as shrimp, or do not feed at all. Once a dwarf male finds a female he hangs on by his jaws. In some anglers, the male's whole body fuses with hers so he receives food via her bloodstream.

Big, stretchy stomach allows deep sea anglerfish to take huge meals

Extraordinary eyes look like binoculars

Model of *Gigantura*

TOUGH JELLY

Found in all the world's oceans, *Atolla* jellyfish are as tough as fruit gums. The reddish-brown colour is typical of deep sea jellyfish. Like most jellyfish, they have stinging tentacles to catch prey. If disturbed, *Atolla* glows in the dark, sending out a bluish light for several seconds.

On the bottom

THE BOTTOM OF THE DEEP OCEAN is not an easy place to live. There is little food and it is dark and cold. Much of the sea bed is covered with soft clays or mud-like oozes made of skeletons of tiny sea animals and plants. The ooze on the vast open plains of the abyss can reach several hundred metres thick. Animals walking along the bottom have long legs to avoid stirring it up. Some grow anchored to the sea bed and have long stems to keep their feeding structures clear of the ooze. Food particles can be filtered out of the water, for example, by the feathery arms in sea lilies or through the many pores in sponges. Some animals, such as sea cucumbers, feed on the sea bed and manage to extract enough goodness from food particles within the ooze. Food particles are the remains of dead animals (and their droppings) and plants that have sunk down from above. Occasionally, a larger carcass reaches the bottom uneaten, providing a real bonanza for the mobile bottom dwellers which home in on it from all around. Because food is scarce and temperatures so low, most animals living in the deep ocean take a long time to grow.

Underwater cables were laid across the Atlantic Ocean to relay telegraphic messages, c. 1870

Dried remains of sea anemones

GLASSY STRANDS
This sponge grows anchored to the soft sea bed by its stem of glass strands and sea anemones often grow on their stems. When a glass-rope sponge dies, the cup-shaped part disappears and all that is left is the stem stuck in the sea bed.

Stem formed by long, glassy, needle-like spikes made of silica

NOT A TRUE SPIDER
Looking like land spiders, sea spiders belong to a group called pycnogonids. Some deep-sea spiders have a leg span of 60 cm (2 ft) across, and can stride along without stirring up clouds of particles. They can also swim, by launching off the sea bed, bringing their legs upwards, then sinking down again.

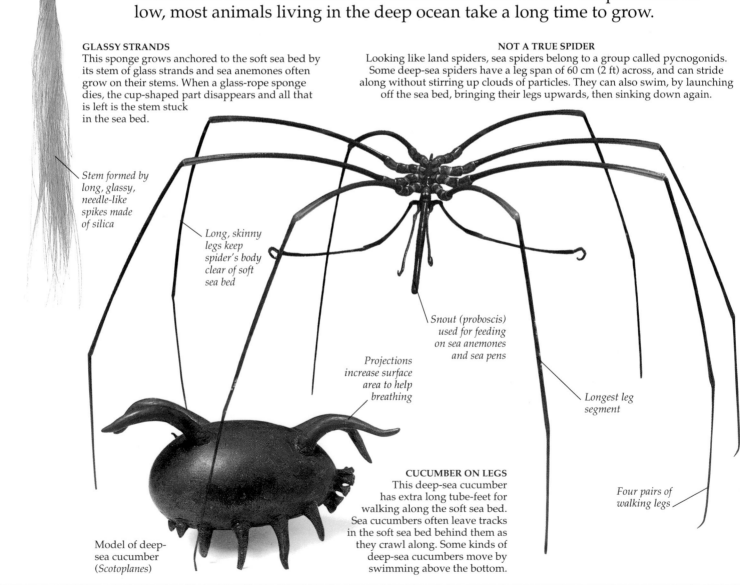

Long, skinny legs keep spider's body clear of soft sea bed

Snout (proboscis) used for feeding on sea anemones and sea pens

Projections increase surface area to help breathing

Longest leg segment

CUCUMBER ON LEGS
This deep-sea cucumber has extra long tube-feet for walking along the soft sea bed. Sea cucumbers often leave tracks in the soft sea bed behind them as they crawl along. Some kinds of deep-sea cucumbers move by swimming above the bottom.

Four pairs of walking legs

Model of deep-sea cucumber (*Scotoplanes*)

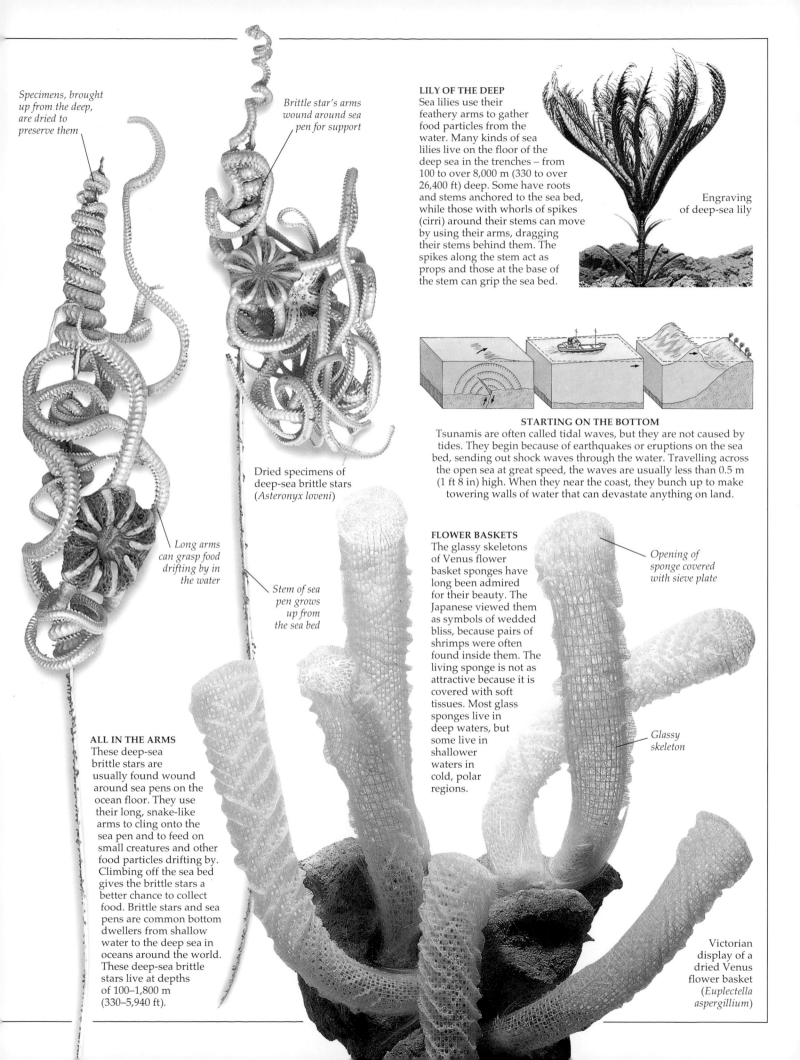

Specimens, brought up from the deep, are dried to preserve them

Brittle star's arms wound around sea pen for support

LILY OF THE DEEP
Sea lilies use their feathery arms to gather food particles from the water. Many kinds of sea lilies live on the floor of the deep sea in the trenches – from 100 to over 8,000 m (330 to over 26,400 ft) deep. Some have roots and stems anchored to the sea bed, while those with whorls of spikes (cirri) around their stems can move by using their arms, dragging their stems behind them. The spikes along the stem act as props and those at the base of the stem can grip the sea bed.

Engraving of deep-sea lily

Dried specimens of deep-sea brittle stars (Asteronyx loveni)

Long arms can grasp food drifting by in the water

Stem of sea pen grows up from the sea bed

STARTING ON THE BOTTOM
Tsunamis are often called tidal waves, but they are not caused by tides. They begin because of earthquakes or eruptions on the sea bed, sending out shock waves through the water. Travelling across the open sea at great speed, the waves are usually less than 0.5 m (1 ft 8 in) high. When they near the coast, they bunch up to make towering walls of water that can devastate anything on land.

FLOWER BASKETS
The glassy skeletons of Venus flower basket sponges have long been admired for their beauty. The Japanese viewed them as symbols of wedded bliss, because pairs of shrimps were often found inside them. The living sponge is not as attractive because it is covered with soft tissues. Most glass sponges live in deep waters, but some live in shallower waters in cold, polar regions.

Opening of sponge covered with sieve plate

Glassy skeleton

ALL IN THE ARMS
These deep-sea brittle stars are usually found wound around sea pens on the ocean floor. They use their long, snake-like arms to cling onto the sea pen and to feed on small creatures and other food particles drifting by. Climbing off the sea bed gives the brittle stars a better chance to collect food. Brittle stars and sea pens are common bottom dwellers from shallow water to the deep sea in oceans around the world. These deep-sea brittle stars live at depths of 100–1,800 m (330–5,940 ft).

Victorian display of a dried Venus flower basket (Euplectella aspergillium)

Vents and smokers

In parts of the ocean floor, there are cracks from which very hot, mineral-rich water gushes. These vents, or hot springs, exist at the spreading centres where gigantic plates which make up the earth's crust are moving apart. Cold seawater sinks deep into cracks in the crust where the water is heated, collecting dissolved minerals. At temperatures of up to 400°C (752°F), hot water spews out and some of the minerals form chimneys (black smokers). Hot water produced by vents helps bacteria to grow, which create food from the hydrogen sulphide in the water. Extraordinary animals crowd around the cracks and rely on these microbes for food. In the late 1970s, scientists using submersibles discovered the first vent communities in the Pacific. Since then, vents have been discovered in other spreading centres in the Pacific and the Mid-Atlantic Ridge.

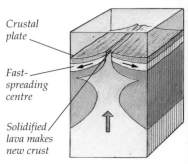

Crustal plate

Fast-spreading centre

Solidified lava makes new crust

GROWING OCEAN
New areas of ocean floor are continually being created at spreading centres between two crustal plates. When hot, molten rock (lava) emerges from within the crust, it cools and solidifies adding material to the edge of each adjoining plate. Old areas of ocean floor are destroyed where one plate slides under another. Lava from volcanic eruptions at spreading centres can kill off communities of vent animals.

Animals cook if too close to hot water in a vent

Plumes of hot water are rich in sulphides, which are poisonous to most animals

Fish predators nibble tops off tube worms

Dense numbers of animals crowd round a vent

BLACK SMOKER
Animal life abounds in an active vent site, such as this one in the Mid-Atlantic Ridge. If the vent stops producing hot, sulphur-rich water, the community is doomed. Animals from dying vents must colonize a new site, which may be several hundred kilometres away across the cold, almost foodless sea floor.

Giant clams in the eastern Pacific can grow to 30 cm (12 in) long

Some animals graze on mats of bacteria covering rocks near a vent

Model of hydrothermal vents found in the eastern Pacific

Deep-sea fish photographed from Alvin near a vent on the Mid-Atlantic Ridge

Alvin by the support ship, Atlantis II

Black smoker chimney can reach 10 m (33 ft) high

Chimney made from mineral deposits

CHAMPION SUBMERSIBLE

The US submersible, *Alvin*, was the first to take scientists down to observe marine life near the Galapagos vents in the east Pacific in the 1970s. Since then, *Alvin* has completed many dives to vents around the world to depths of 3,800 m (12,500 ft). Other submersibles that have dived on vent sites include the French *Nautile* (pp. 54–55) and the Russian *Mirs I* and *II*.

VENT COMMUNITIES

This model shows the vent communities in the eastern Pacific, where giant clams and tube worms are the most distinctive animals. Vents in other parts of the world have different groups of animals, such as the hairy snails from the Mariana Trench and eyeless shrimps from vents along the Mid-Atlantic Ridge.

Tube worm can grow to 3 m (10 ft) long

Giant tube worm has bacteria inside its body, which provides the worm with food

Diverse divers

PEOPLE HAVE ALWAYS WANTED to explore the sea, to look for sunken treasure, to salvage wrecks, to bring up marine products like pearls and sponges, or to examine the beautiful underwater world. Recently, underwater oil exploration and drilling have also required divers' skills. The first diving equipment were simple bells, containing air and open at the bottom so the diver could work on the sea bed. Later, diving suits with hard helmets were invented to enable divers to go deeper and stay down longer, with air pumped continually down a line from the surface. In the 1940s, the modern aqualung or SCUBA (Self-Contained, Underwater Breathing Apparatus) was invented. Divers could carry their own supply of compressed air in tanks on their backs.

Umbilical supplies air and electricity for light

Weight belt

UNDERWATER WORKER
This diver, wearing a wetsuit for warmth, gets air into the helmet via a line linked to the surface. A harness goes round the diver's middle to carry tools. Flexible boots help the diver clamber around beneath an oil rig.

Rope connecting bell to surface

Wooden bell

Weight

EARLY DIVING BELL
In 1690, Edmund Halley invented a diving bell, allowing a diver to be resupplied with barrels of air lowered from the surface. Open at the bottom, heavy weights anchored the bell to the sea bed. A leather tube connected the lead-lined air barrel to the wooden bell. Used at depths of 18 m (60 ft), several divers at a time could work from the bell.

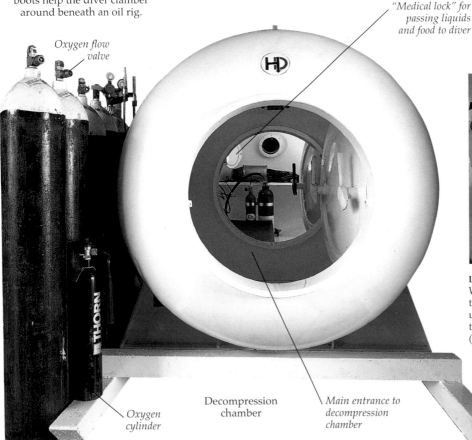

Oxygen flow valve

"Medical lock" for passing liquids and food to diver

Joint pains indicate decompression sickness

Oxygen cylinder

Decompression chamber

Main entrance to decompression chamber

LIFE SAVER
When diving, the pressure on the body increases due to the weight of water above the diver. The air is supplied under the same pressure so the diver can breathe. With this increased pressure, the nitrogen in the air supply (air contains 80 per cent nitrogen) passes into the blood. If a diver comes up too quickly after a long or deep dive, the sudden release of pressure can cause nitrogen to form bubbles in the blood and tissues. This painful, sometimes fatal condition is called decompression sickness (the bends). The ailing diver is treated in a decompression chamber. The pressure is raised to the level required to move bubbles out through the lungs, and then is slowly reduced to normal pressure at the surface.

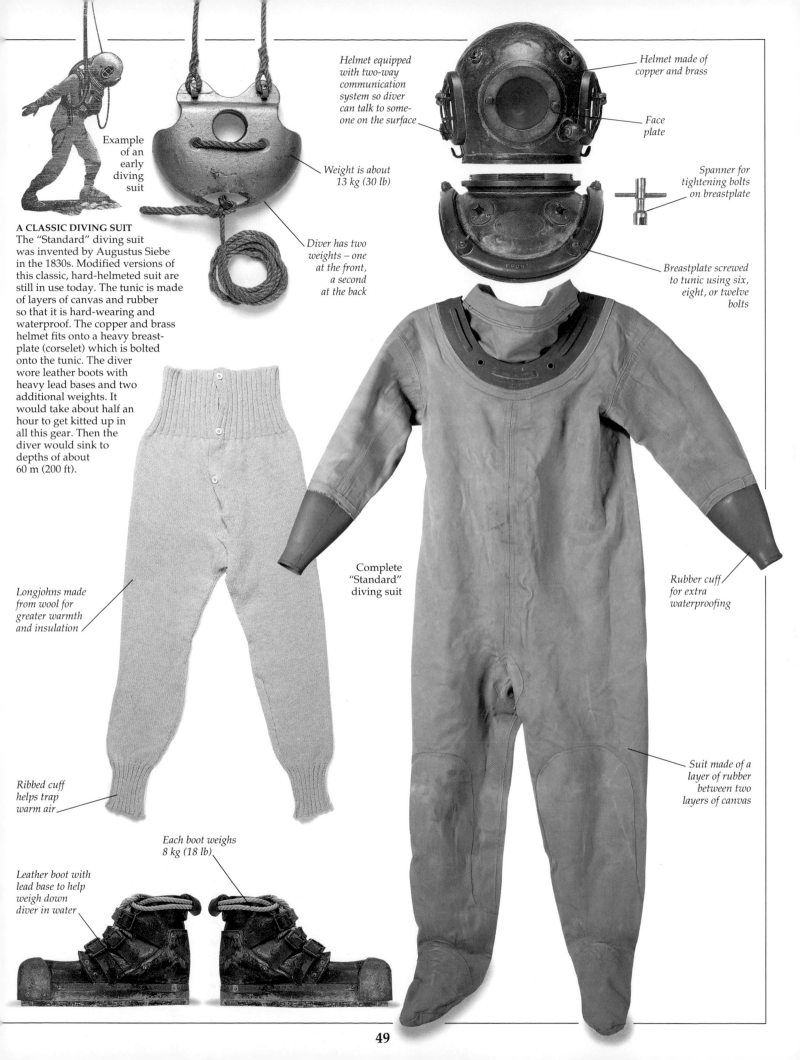

Example of an early diving suit

A CLASSIC DIVING SUIT
The "Standard" diving suit was invented by Augustus Siebe in the 1830s. Modified versions of this classic, hard-helmeted suit are still in use today. The tunic is made of layers of canvas and rubber so that it is hard-wearing and waterproof. The copper and brass helmet fits onto a heavy breast-plate (corselet) which is bolted onto the tunic. The diver wore leather boots with heavy lead bases and two additional weights. It would take about half an hour to get kitted up in all this gear. Then the diver would sink to depths of about 60 m (200 ft).

Helmet equipped with two-way communication system so diver can talk to some-one on the surface

Weight is about 13 kg (30 lb)

Diver has two weights – one at the front, a second at the back

Helmet made of copper and brass

Face plate

Spanner for tightening bolts on breastplate

Breastplate screwed to tunic using six, eight, or twelve bolts

Complete "Standard" diving suit

Rubber cuff for extra waterproofing

Longjohns made from wool for greater warmth and insulation

Ribbed cuff helps trap warm air

Suit made of a layer of rubber between two layers of canvas

Each boot weighs 8 kg (18 lb)

Leather boot with lead base to help weigh down diver in water

Underwater machines

THE FIRST SUBMARINES were simple designs. They allowed travel underwater and were useful in war. More modern submarines were powered by diesel or petrol while on the surface and used batteries underwater. In 1955, the first submarine run on nuclear fuel traversed the oceans. Nuclear power allowed submarines to travel great distances before needing to refuel. Today, submarines have sophisticated sonar systems for navigating underwater and pinpointing other vessels. They can carry high-powered torpedoes to fire at enemy craft or nuclear missiles. Submersibles (miniature submarines), used to explore the deep sea floor, cannot travel long distances. They need to be lowered from a support vessel on the surface.

Snort mast to renew and expel air with help of bellows

Augur for drilling into enemy ship to attach mine on rope

Delayed action mine

Vertical propeller

Side propeller powered by foot pedals

"TURTLE" HERO
A one-man wooden submarine, the *Turtle*, was used during the American Revolutionary War in 1776 to attach a delayed-action mine to an English ship blockading New York Harbour. The operator became disorientated by carbon dioxide building up inside the *Turtle* and the mine struck metal instead of the ship's wooden hull. Both the ship and operator survived, but the mine was jettisoned.

UNDERWATER ADVENTURE
Inspired by the invention of modern submarines, this 1900 engraving depicted a scene in the year 2000 with people enjoying a journey in a submarine liner. In a way, the prediction has come true as tourists can now take trips in small submarines to view marine life in places such as the Red Sea. However, most people explore the underwater world by learning to scuba dive or snorkel.

External steering bar operated by diver

Internal steering position

Hand pump for pressurizing air reservoir and emptying ballast tanks

Front wheels smaller than back ones for easier turning

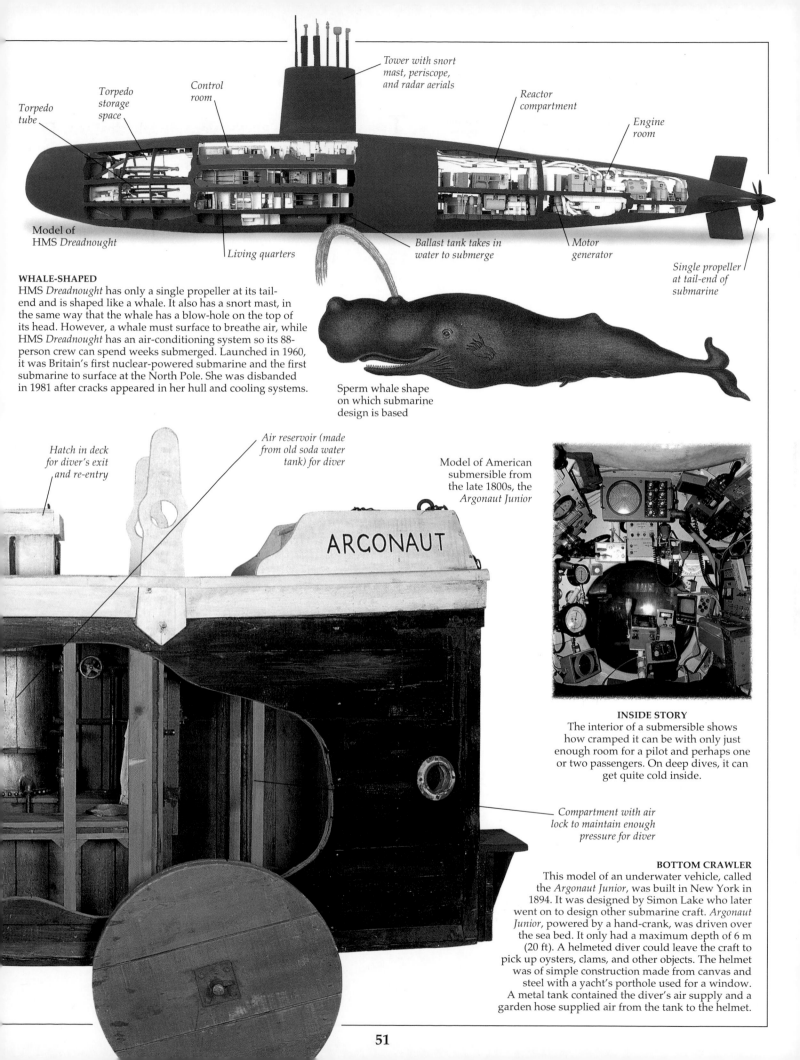

Tower with snort mast, periscope, and radar aerials

Control room

Torpedo storage space

Torpedo tube

Reactor compartment

Engine room

Model of HMS Dreadnought

Living quarters

Ballast tank takes in water to submerge

Motor generator

Single propeller at tail-end of submarine

WHALE-SHAPED

HMS Dreadnought has only a single propeller at its tail-end and is shaped like a whale. It also has a snort mast, in the same way that the whale has a blow-hole on the top of its head. However, a whale must surface to breathe air, while HMS Dreadnought has an air-conditioning system so its 88-person crew can spend weeks submerged. Launched in 1960, it was Britain's first nuclear-powered submarine and the first submarine to surface at the North Pole. She was disbanded in 1981 after cracks appeared in her hull and cooling systems.

Sperm whale shape on which submarine design is based

Hatch in deck for diver's exit and re-entry

Air reservoir (made from old soda water tank) for diver

Model of American submersible from the late 1800s, the Argonaut Junior

ARGONAUT

INSIDE STORY

The interior of a submersible shows how cramped it can be with only just enough room for a pilot and perhaps one or two passengers. On deep dives, it can get quite cold inside.

Compartment with air lock to maintain enough pressure for diver

BOTTOM CRAWLER

This model of an underwater vehicle, called the Argonaut Junior, was built in New York in 1894. It was designed by Simon Lake who later went on to design other submarine craft. Argonaut Junior, powered by a hand-crank, was driven over the sea bed. It only had a maximum depth of 6 m (20 ft). A helmeted diver could leave the craft to pick up oysters, clams, and other objects. The helmet was of simple construction made from canvas and steel with a yacht's porthole used for a window. A metal tank contained the diver's air supply and a garden hose supplied air from the tank to the helmet.

Ocean explorers

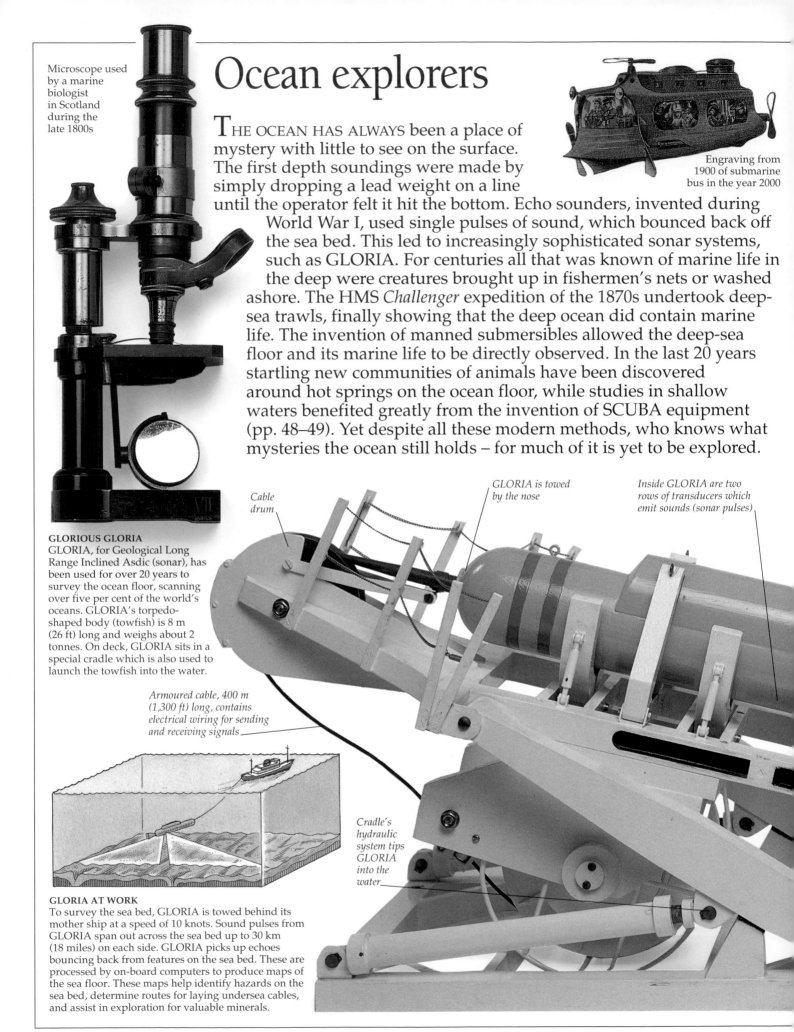

Microscope used by a marine biologist in Scotland during the late 1800s

Engraving from 1900 of submarine bus in the year 2000

THE OCEAN HAS ALWAYS been a place of mystery with little to see on the surface. The first depth soundings were made by simply dropping a lead weight on a line until the operator felt it hit the bottom. Echo sounders, invented during World War I, used single pulses of sound, which bounced back off the sea bed. This led to increasingly sophisticated sonar systems, such as GLORIA. For centuries all that was known of marine life in the deep were creatures brought up in fishermen's nets or washed ashore. The HMS *Challenger* expedition of the 1870s undertook deep-sea trawls, finally showing that the deep ocean did contain marine life. The invention of manned submersibles allowed the deep-sea floor and its marine life to be directly observed. In the last 20 years startling new communities of animals have been discovered around hot springs on the ocean floor, while studies in shallow waters benefited greatly from the invention of SCUBA equipment (pp. 48–49). Yet despite all these modern methods, who knows what mysteries the ocean still holds – for much of it is yet to be explored.

GLORIOUS GLORIA
GLORIA, for Geological Long Range Inclined Asdic (sonar), has been used for over 20 years to survey the ocean floor, scanning over five per cent of the world's oceans. GLORIA's torpedo-shaped body (towfish) is 8 m (26 ft) long and weighs about 2 tonnes. On deck, GLORIA sits in a special cradle which is also used to launch the towfish into the water.

Cable drum

GLORIA is towed by the nose

Inside GLORIA are two rows of transducers which emit sounds (sonar pulses)

Armoured cable, 400 m (1,300 ft) long, contains electrical wiring for sending and receiving signals

Cradle's hydraulic system tips GLORIA into the water

GLORIA AT WORK
To survey the sea bed, GLORIA is towed behind its mother ship at a speed of 10 knots. Sound pulses from GLORIA span out across the sea bed up to 30 km (18 miles) on each side. GLORIA picks up echoes bouncing back from features on the sea bed. These are processed by on-board computers to produce maps of the sea floor. These maps help identify hazards on the sea bed, determine routes for laying undersea cables, and assist in exploration for valuable minerals.

SNORKELLING

A simple way to observe life underwater is to snorkel. The snorkel goes under the strap of the face mask and sticks out above the water. By breathing in through the mouthpiece, air is drawn down the snorkel and air is expelled through the snorkel by breathing out.

Diver looking at grouper fish in the Red Sea

Air expelled through end of snorkel

Flippers propel swimmer along, but arms should be kept near the body for streamlining

Face mask traps air to let swimmer view life in the water

Swimmer breathes in air and expels it out through mouthpiece

Snorkel tube

SCUBA DIVING

Use of scuba equipment has proved invaluable in the study of marine life in shallow waters. Instead of bringing animals into an aquarium, marine biologists can observe them in the wild. Some animals, such as hammerhead sharks, are sensitive to the noises made by air bubbles and may be scared away.

Flippers used in snorkelling and SCUBA diving

Rope guide, used during recovery of GLORIA

Deep Star can reach depths of 1,200 m (4,000 ft)

DEEP STARS

Many different submersibles have been used for underwater exploration (left). The deepest dive ever was to 10,911 m (35,800 ft) in the Mariana Trench by the Swiss Jacques Piccard (1922–) in his bathyscaphe in 1960. Another famous dive (in 1934 by the Americans Barton and Beebe) was in a bathysphere.

GLORIA covers 20,000 sq km (7,700 sq miles) in a day

Launching cradle weighs about 13 tonnes

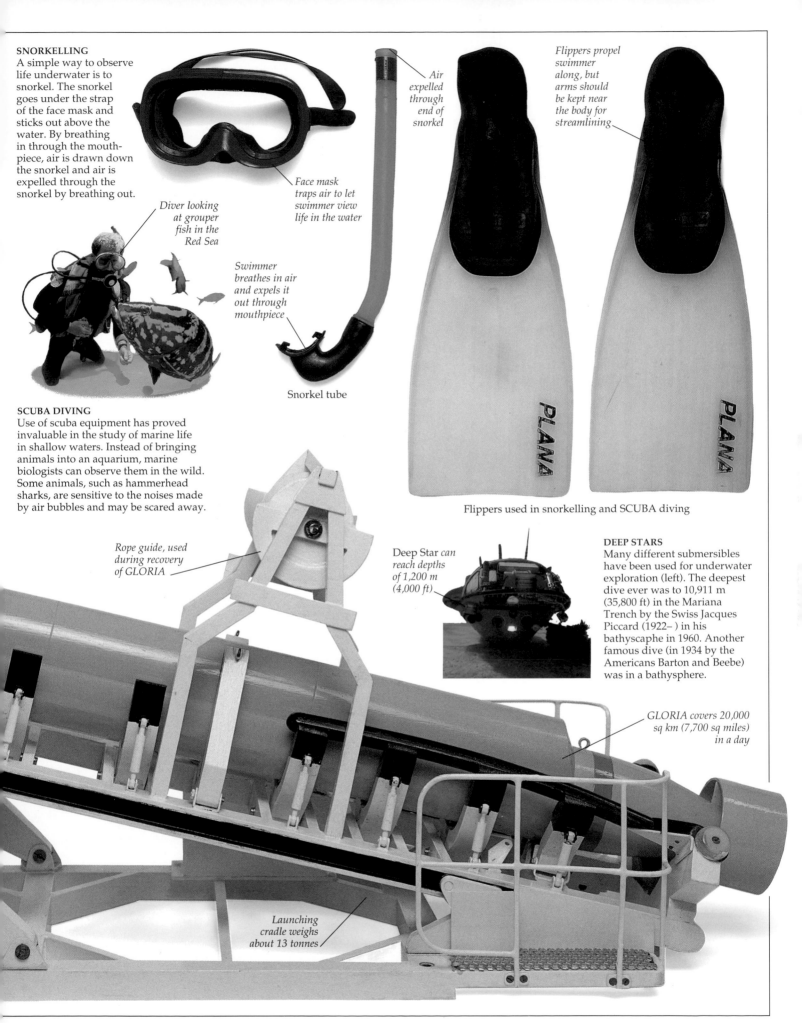

Wrecks on the sea bed

Ever since people took to the sea in boats, there have been wrecks on the sea bed. Mud and sand cover wooden boats, preserving them for centuries. This sediment protects the timbers by keeping out the oxygen which speeds up decay. Metal-hulled ships are badly corroded by seawater. The *Titanic*'s steel hull could disintegrate within a hundred years. Wrecks in shallow water get covered by plant and animal life, turning them into living reefs. Apart from animals, such as corals and sponges growing on the outside, fish shelter inside as if in an underwater cave. Wrecks and their objects tell us much about life in the past, but archaeologists must first survey them carefully. Objects brought up are washed clean of salt and sometimes treated with chemicals to preserve them. Treasure seekers, unfortunately, can do much damage.

Less valuable silver coin

GLITTERING GOLD
Gold is among the most sought after treasure. These Spanish coins, much in demand by pirates, sometimes ended up on the sea bed when a ship sunk.

Sonar equipment

Titanium sphere protects passengers

IFREMI
DCN CERTS

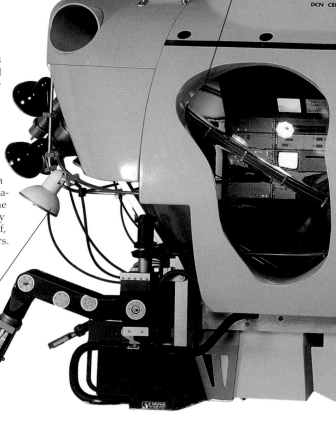

SUPER SUB
The French submersible, *Nautile*, recovered objects from the sea bed surrounding the wreck of the *Titanic*. When the ship went down, it broke in two, scattering objects far and wide. Only a submersible could dive deep enough to reach the *Titanic*, 3,780 m (2.5 miles) down. With space for only three people (pilot, co-pilot, and an observer), they sit in a sphere made of titanium metal which protects them from the immense pressure at these depths. Extra-thick, curved plexiglass portholes become flat on a dive due to pressure. The journey to the wreck takes about an hour and a half, and *Nautile* can stay down for eight hours.

Lights for video camera

Manipulator arm for picking objects off sea bed

VALUABLE PROPERTY
In 1892, divers worked on the wreck of the tug, *L'Abeille*, which sank off Le Havre, France. For centuries, people have salvaged wrecks to bring up items of value.

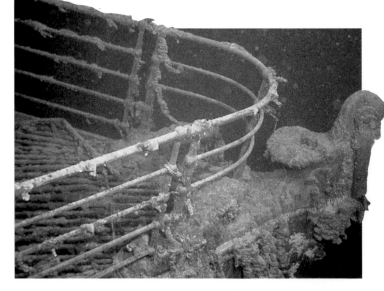

SAD REMINDERS
Many items recovered from the *Titanic* wreck were not valuable, but everyday items used by those aboard. Personal effects, such as buttons or just cutlery, remind us of those who died.

THE UNSINKABLE SHIP
In 1912, the *Titanic* sailed from England to New York on her maiden voyage. Because of her hull's water-tight compartments, she was thought unsinkable, but hit an iceberg four days into the voyage. She took two hours and forty minutes to sink, with only 705 people saved of 2,228. She was discovered in 1985 by a French-US team, using remote-controlled video equipment. The submersibles *Alvin* (USA) and *Mir* (Russia) have also dived to the wreck since then.

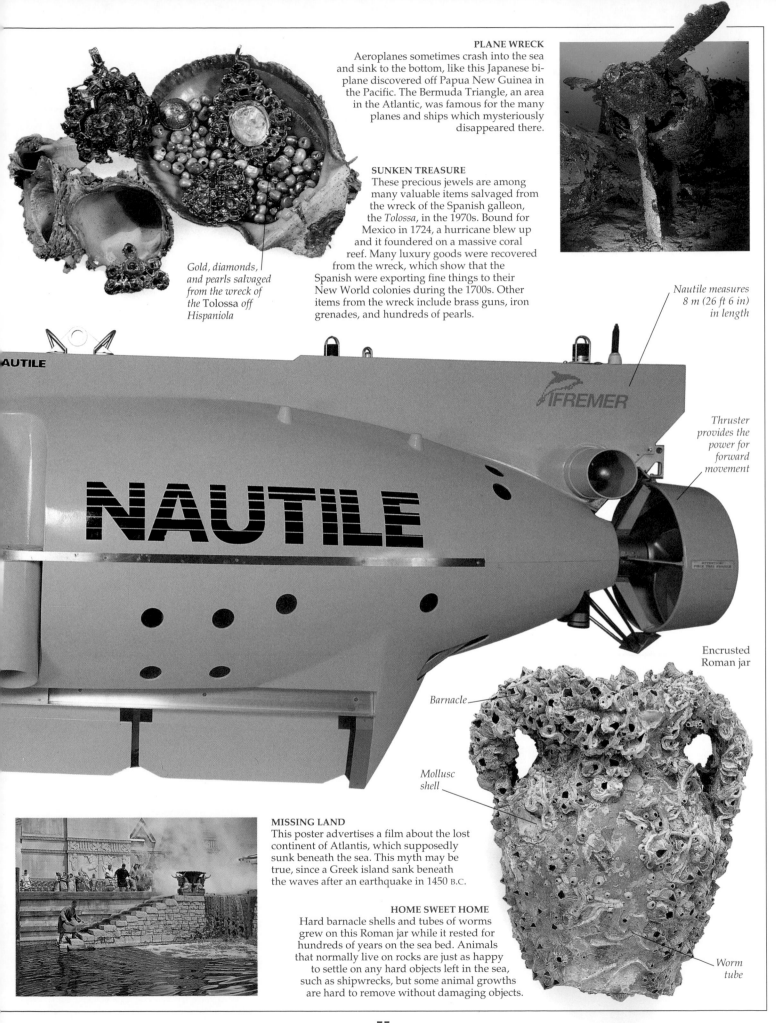

PLANE WRECK
Aeroplanes sometimes crash into the sea and sink to the bottom, like this Japanese bi-plane discovered off Papua New Guinea in the Pacific. The Bermuda Triangle, an area in the Atlantic, was famous for the many planes and ships which mysteriously disappeared there.

SUNKEN TREASURE
These precious jewels are among many valuable items salvaged from the wreck of the Spanish galleon, the *Tolossa*, in the 1970s. Bound for Mexico in 1724, a hurricane blew up and it foundered on a massive coral reef. Many luxury goods were recovered from the wreck, which show that the Spanish were exporting fine things to their New World colonies during the 1700s. Other items from the wreck include brass guns, iron grenades, and hundreds of pearls.

Gold, diamonds, and pearls salvaged from the wreck of the Tolossa *off Hispaniola*

Nautile measures 8 m (26 ft 6 in) in length

Thruster provides the power for forward movement

AUTILE

IFREMER

NAUTILE

Encrusted Roman jar

Barnacle

Mollusc shell

MISSING LAND
This poster advertises a film about the lost continent of Atlantis, which supposedly sunk beneath the sea. This myth may be true, since a Greek island sank beneath the waves after an earthquake in 1450 B.C.

HOME SWEET HOME
Hard barnacle shells and tubes of worms grew on this Roman jar while it rested for hundreds of years on the sea bed. Animals that normally live on rocks are just as happy to settle on any hard objects left in the sea, such as shipwrecks, but some animal growths are hard to remove without damaging objects.

Worm tube

Harvesting fish

FISH ARE THE MOST popular kind of sea food, with some 70 million tonnes (68.9 million tons) caught around the world each year. Some fish are caught by hand-thrown nets and traps in local waters, but far more are caught at sea by modern fishing vessels with the latest technology. Some fish are caught on long lines with many hooks or ensnared when they swim into long walls of drift nets. Bottom-dwelling fish are trawled or whole shoals are gathered up in huge nets set in mid-water. Using sonar to detect shoals means there are few places where fish can escape notice. Even fish living in deep waters, such as orange roughy at depths of 1,000 m (3,300 ft), are brought up in numbers. Many people are concerned that too many fish are being caught because numbers take a long time to recover. Competition for fish stocks is fierce and it is difficult for fishermen to make a living. But some fish, such as salmon, are farmed to help meet demands.

1 HATCHING OUT
Salmon begin life in rivers and streams where they hatch from eggs laid in a shallow hollow among gravel. First the fry (alevins) grow, using the contents of their egg sac attached to their bellies as food.

2 YOUNG SALMON
At a few weeks old, the egg sac disappears, so young salmon must feed on tiny insects in the river. Soon dark spots appear on the young salmon (called parr). The parr stay in the river for a year or more, before turning into silvery smolt which head for the sea.

3 AT SEA
Atlantic salmon spend up to four years at sea, feeding on other fishes. They grow rapidly, putting on several kilos annually. Then the mature salmon return to their home rivers and streams where they hatch. They recognize their home stream by a number of clues, including its "smell" (particular combinations of tiny quantities of substances in the water).

Fin rays are well-developed

Large, first dorsal fin

Pelvic fin

Pectoral fin

Operculum (flap covering gills)

Mouth for feeding and taking in water to "breathe"

FISH FARMING
Salmon are among the few kinds of sea fish to be farmed successfully. Young salmon are reared in fresh water. When large enough, they are released into floating pens in the sea. These are located in relatively calm waters, such as sea lochs, so the fish are not washed away. To help them grow quickly, the salmon are fed regularly with dried fish pellets. Like any farmed animals, care must be taken to stop the salmon developing diseases.

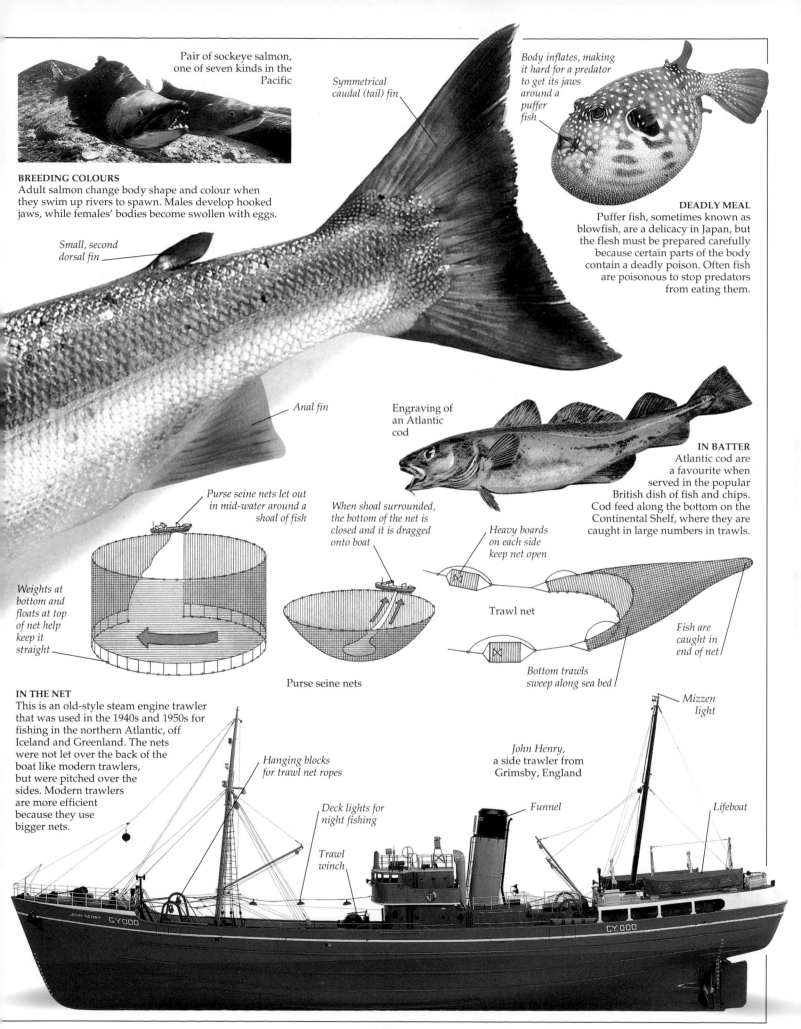

Pair of sockeye salmon, one of seven kinds in the Pacific

Symmetrical caudal (tail) fin

Body inflates, making it hard for a predator to get its jaws around a puffer fish

BREEDING COLOURS
Adult salmon change body shape and colour when they swim up rivers to spawn. Males develop hooked jaws, while females' bodies become swollen with eggs.

Small, second dorsal fin

DEADLY MEAL
Puffer fish, sometimes known as blowfish, are a delicacy in Japan, but the flesh must be prepared carefully because certain parts of the body contain a deadly poison. Often fish are poisonous to stop predators from eating them.

Anal fin

Engraving of an Atlantic cod

IN BATTER
Atlantic cod are a favourite when served in the popular British dish of fish and chips. Cod feed along the bottom on the Continental Shelf, where they are caught in large numbers in trawls.

Purse seine nets let out in mid-water around a shoal of fish

When shoal surrounded, the bottom of the net is closed and it is dragged onto boat

Heavy boards on each side keep net open

Weights at bottom and floats at top of net help keep it straight

Trawl net

Fish are caught in end of net

Purse seine nets

Bottom trawls sweep along sea bed

IN THE NET
This is an old-style steam engine trawler that was used in the 1940s and 1950s for fishing in the northern Atlantic, off Iceland and Greenland. The nets were not let over the back of the boat like modern trawlers, but were pitched over the sides. Modern trawlers are more efficient because they use bigger nets.

Mizzen light

John Henry, a side trawler from Grimsby, England

Hanging blocks for trawl net ropes

Funnel

Lifeboat

Deck lights for night fishing

Trawl winch

JOHN HENRY GY.000

GY.000

Ocean products

PEOPLE HAVE ALWAYS HARVESTED plants and animals from the ocean. Many different animals are collected for food, from fish, crustaceans (shrimps, lobsters), and molluscs (clams, squid) to more unusual foods, such as sea cucumbers, barnacles, and jellyfish. Seaweeds are eaten too, either in a recognizable state or as an ingredient of ice creams and other processed foods. The products made from sea creatures are amazing, although many (such as mother-of-pearl buttons and sponges) now are replaced by synthetic materials. Yet the appeal of natural ocean products is so great, that some sea animals and certain kinds of seaweeds are cultivated. Among sea creatures to be farmed are giant clams (for pretty shells), mussels (for food), and pearl oysters. Farming is one way to meet demand for products, and to avoid over-collecting the ocean's wildlife.

Yarn dyed purple from pigment of sea snails

ROYAL PURPLE
Sea snails were used to make purple dye for clothes worn by kings in ancient times. Making dye was a smelly process, as huge quantities of salted snails were left in vats gouged out of rocks. The purple liquid was collected and heated to concentrate the dye. These sea snails (from Florida and the Caribbean) are used to make purple dye.

Slate-pencil sea urchin from tropical coral reefs in the Indo-Pacific

Short, blunt spines surround mouth

USEFUL SPINES
The spines of this urchin were once used as pencils to write on slate boards. Slate-pencil urchins are still collected, their spines used for wind chimes. Hung from threads, the spines clink together when the wind blows through them. Urchins use their big spines to help them walk across the sea bed, when they emerge from crevices to feed at night.

Long, very strong spines help protect urchin from predators

Spines help urchin move and to hold it in place

Five, strong white teeth protrude from urchin's mouth (viewed from underneath)

Soft skeleton left after processing living sponge

SOFT SKELETON
Bath sponges, harvested from the sandy sea bed, grow among sea grasses in reef lagoons. When brought up from the bottom, the sponges are covered with slimy, living tissues. Mainly collected from the Mediterranean, Caribbean, and Pacific, natural sponges are prone to diseases and over-collecting.

SEAWEED FARM
In Japan, seaweeds are used in crackers and to wrap raw fish parcels. Red seaweed is grown in the sea on bamboo poles, collected, and dried. Laver, a similar kind of red seaweed is eaten in Wales, UK. Made from red seaweeds, agar (a jelly-like substance) is used in foods and in medical research. Seaweeds are also used as fertilizers.

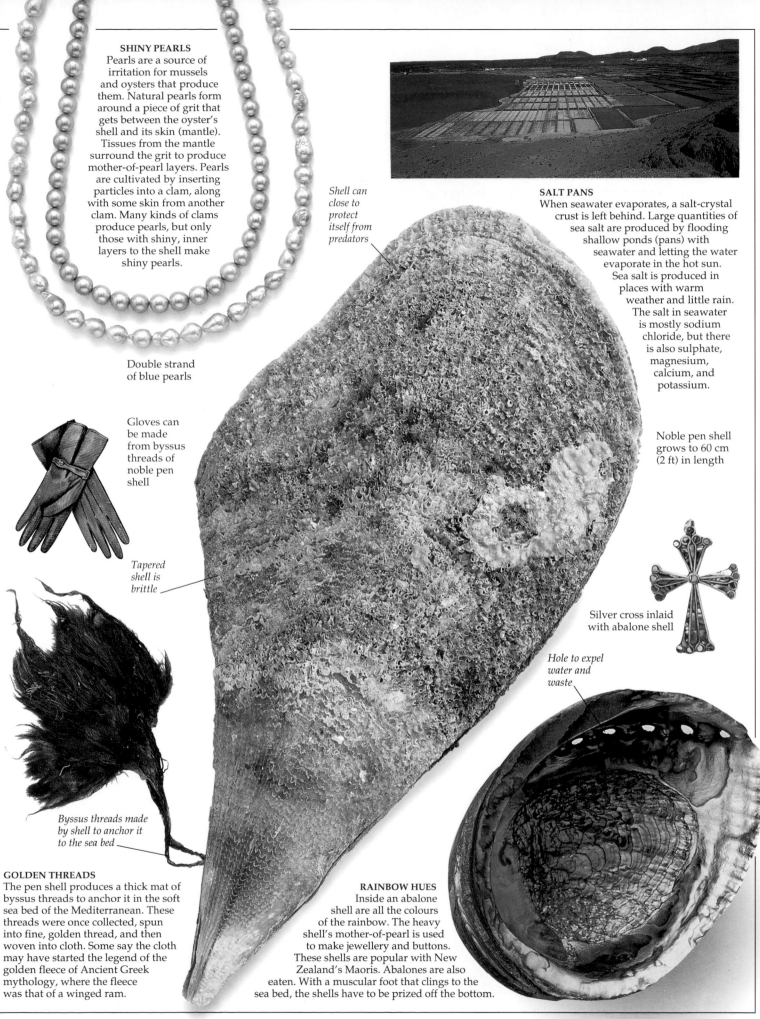

SHINY PEARLS
Pearls are a source of irritation for mussels and oysters that produce them. Natural pearls form around a piece of grit that gets between the oyster's shell and its skin (mantle). Tissues from the mantle surround the grit to produce mother-of-pearl layers. Pearls are cultivated by inserting particles into a clam, along with some skin from another clam. Many kinds of clams produce pearls, but only those with shiny, inner layers to the shell make shiny pearls.

Shell can close to protect itself from predators

SALT PANS
When seawater evaporates, a salt-crystal crust is left behind. Large quantities of sea salt are produced by flooding shallow ponds (pans) with seawater and letting the water evaporate in the hot sun. Sea salt is produced in places with warm weather and little rain. The salt in seawater is mostly sodium chloride, but there is also sulphate, magnesium, calcium, and potassium.

Double strand of blue pearls

Gloves can be made from byssus threads of noble pen shell

Noble pen shell grows to 60 cm (2 ft) in length

Tapered shell is brittle

Silver cross inlaid with abalone shell

Hole to expel water and waste

Byssus threads made by shell to anchor it to the sea bed

GOLDEN THREADS
The pen shell produces a thick mat of byssus threads to anchor it in the soft sea bed of the Mediterranean. These threads were once collected, spun into fine, golden thread, and then woven into cloth. Some say the cloth may have started the legend of the golden fleece of Ancient Greek mythology, where the fleece was that of a winged ram.

RAINBOW HUES
Inside an abalone shell are all the colours of the rainbow. The heavy shell's mother-of-pearl is used to make jewellery and buttons. These shells are popular with New Zealand's Maoris. Abalones are also eaten. With a muscular foot that clings to the sea bed, the shells have to be prized off the bottom.

Oil and gas exploration

V ALUABLE RESERVOIRS OF OIL AND GAS lie hidden in rocks on the sea bed. Oil and gas are tapped by drilling down through the rocks, but first geologists must know where to drill. Only certain kinds of rocks hold oil and gas, but must be in shallow enough water to be reached by drilling. Geologists find the reservoirs by sending shock waves through the sea bed and using the returning signals to distinguish between the rock layers. Temporary rigs are set up to pinpoint a source to see if the oil is the right quality and quantity. To extract oil or gas, the rig is replaced by a more permanent oil platform, which is firmly anchored to the sea bed. Oil is off-loaded from separate storage tanks into larger tankers or sent via pipelines ashore. When reservoirs dry up, new sources have to be found as there is a great demand for energy, but the earth's supplies of oil and gas are limited. The main offshore oil fields are in the North Sea, Gulf of Mexico, Persian Gulf, and along the coasts of South America and Asia.

ON FIRE
Oil and gas are highly flammable. Despite precautions, accidents do happen, like the North Sea's Piper Alpha disaster in 1988 when 167 people died. Since then safety measures have been improved.

MILK ROUND
Helicopters deliver supplies to oil platforms far out at sea. Up to 400 people can live and work on an oil platform, but fly by helicopter for breaks on shore every few weeks.

OIL PLATFORM
One of the smaller oil platforms in the North Sea has concrete legs. Platforms are built in sections on shore. The largest section is towed out to sea and tipped upright onto the sea bed, then living quarters are added. A tall derrick holds drilling equipment – several pipes tipped with a strong drill bit for grinding the rocks. Special mud is sent down the pipes to cool the drill bit, wash out ground-up rock, and prevent oil gushing out. Oil platforms extract oil or gas, but rigs drill wells during exploration.

Tallest structure on this platform is flare stack for safety reasons

Flare stack for burning off any gas that rises with the oil and cannot be used

Derrick (a steel tower) holds drilling equipment

Fireproof lifeboat gives better chance of survival

Hand rail to protect personnel

Crane hoists supplies up to platform from ship

Helicopter brings fresh food and milk to the platform

Living quarters

Helicopter pad

DEATH AND DECAY
Plant and bacteria remains from ancient seas fell to the sea floor and were covered by mud layers. Heat and pressure turned them into oil, then gas, which moved up through porous rocks, to be trapped by impermeable rocks.

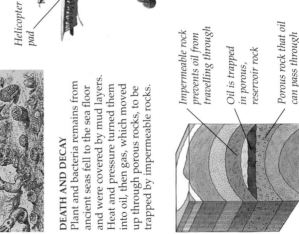

Impermeable rock prevents oil from travelling through

Oil is trapped in porous, reservoir rock

Porous rock that oil can pass through

Formation of fossil fuels

AT WORK

On an oil platform, some people work on deck operating the drill, while others work inside with computers. Geologists examine rock, oil, and gas samples. Mechanics keep the machinery going. There are also cooks and cleaners to look after the crew.

ON THE BOTTOM

Divers (minus Newt suits) doing repairs underwater, work longer if they return to a pressurized chamber, then back into the sea, without having to decompress after each dive.

Strong structure to withstand buffeting by wind and waves

Oxygen carried in cylinders on the back

NEWT SUIT

Thick-walled suits, like the one above, resist pressure. When underwater, the diver breathes air at normal pressure as if inside a submersible. This means a diver can go deeper without having to undergo decompression. Newt suits (above) are used in oil exploration to depths of 365 m (1,200 ft). Joints in the arms and legs allow the diver to move.

Oceans in peril

Jewellery made of teeth of great white shark, now protected in some areas

THE OCEANS AND THE LIFE THEY SUPPORT are under threat. Sewage and industrial waste are dumped into the oceans and poured from pipelines, carrying with them certain chemicals which can create a dangerous build-up in the food chain. Oil spills smother and poison marine life.

Rubbish dumped at sea can choke a turtle or trap a seabird. Many seabirds and sea mammals drown when caught in abandoned fishing nets. Overharvesting has depleted many ocean animals, from whales to fishes. Even the souvenir trade threatens coral reefs. However, the situation is improving. Now laws help stop ocean pollution, regulations protect marine life, and in underwater parks people can look at ocean life, but not disturb it.

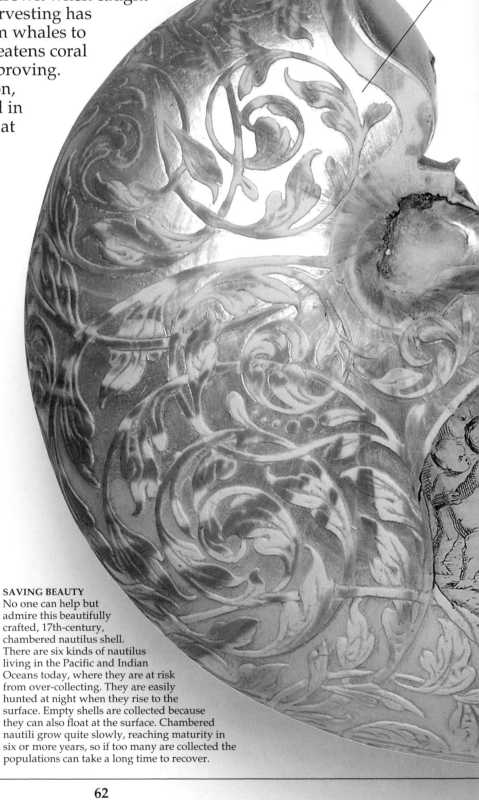

Cut to show mother-of-pearl

HAVE A HEART
Many people collect sea shells, because of their beauty, but most shells sold in shops have been taken as living animals, so if too many shelled creatures are collected from one place, such as a coral reef, the pattern of life can be disrupted. Shells should only be bought if the harvest is properly managed. It is better to go beachcombing and collect shells of already dead creatures. Always check about taking even empty shells, as some nature reserves do not permit this.

Heart cockle shells

OIL SPILL
Oil is needed for industry and motor vehicles. Huge quantities are transported at sea in tankers, sent along pipelines, and brought up from the sea bed. Accidents happen where massive amounts of oil are spilled. Seabirds and sea mammals die of the cold, because their feathers or fur no longer contain pockets of air to keep them warm. Trying to clean themselves, animals die from consuming the oil, which can block their airways. Some are rescued, cleaned, and released back into the wild.

SAVING BEAUTY
No one can help but admire this beautifully crafted, 17th-century, chambered nautilus shell. There are six kinds of nautilus living in the Pacific and Indian Oceans today, where they are at risk from over-collecting. They are easily hunted at night when they rise to the surface. Empty shells are collected because they can also float at the surface. Chambered nautili grow quite slowly, reaching maturity in six or more years, so if too many are collected the populations can take a long time to recover.

WORSE FOR WHALES

For centuries, whales have been hunted for their meat, oil, and bones. Whale oil was used in foods, as lubricants, and in soap and candles, and the broad baleen plates were made into household items such as brushes. The wholesale slaughter by commercial whalers drastically reduced the number of whales. Now most whales are protected, but scientists doubt whether some populations will ever recover their former numbers. Some kinds of whales are still caught for food, mainly by local people.

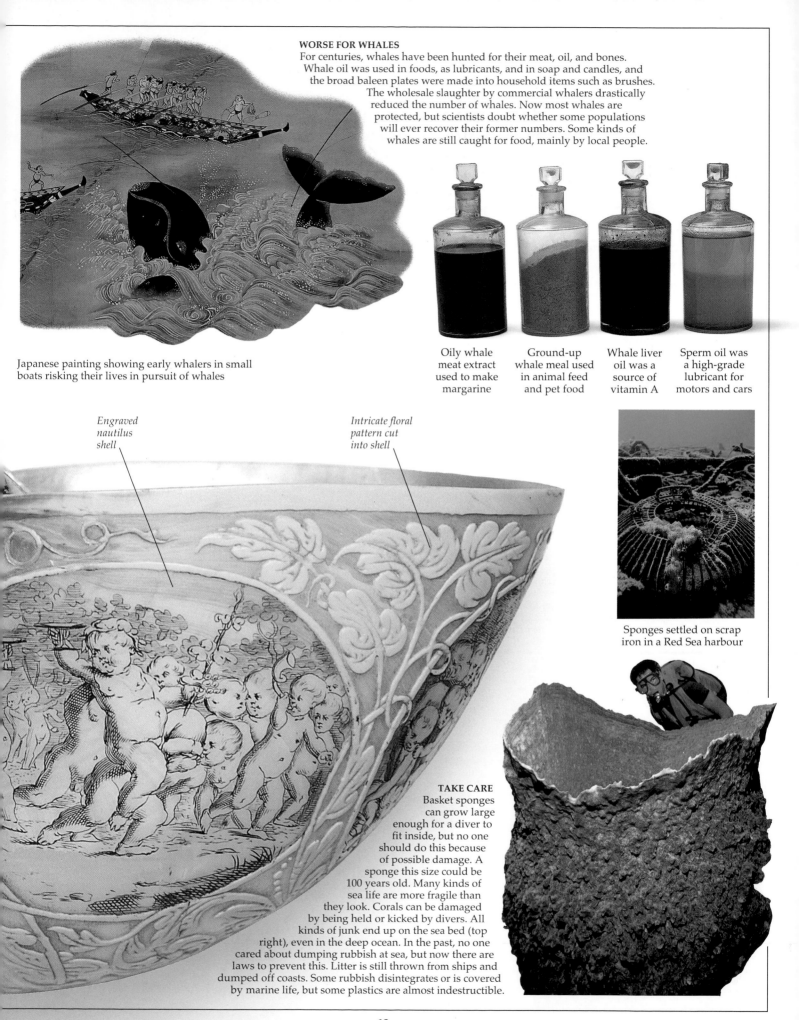

Japanese painting showing early whalers in small boats risking their lives in pursuit of whales

Oily whale meat extract used to make margarine

Ground-up whale meal used in animal feed and pet food

Whale liver oil was a source of vitamin A

Sperm oil was a high-grade lubricant for motors and cars

Engraved nautilus shell

Intricate floral pattern cut into shell

Sponges settled on scrap iron in a Red Sea harbour

TAKE CARE

Basket sponges can grow large enough for a diver to fit inside, but no one should do this because of possible damage. A sponge this size could be 100 years old. Many kinds of sea life are more fragile than they look. Corals can be damaged by being held or kicked by divers. All kinds of junk end up on the sea bed (top right), even in the deep ocean. In the past, no one cared about dumping rubbish at sea, but now there are laws to prevent this. Litter is still thrown from ships and dumped off coasts. Some rubbish disintegrates or is covered by marine life, but some plastics are almost indestructible.

Index

A

abalone 59
Abyssal Plain 9–10, 44–45; Demerara 8; Hatteras 9; Nares 8
algae 20, 22, 24
Alvin 47, 54
anemone, cloak 31; Dahlia 29; sea 10, 20, 22, 24, 28–29, 31, 44
archaeology, underwater 54–55
Argonaut Junior 51
arthropod 10
Asteronyxloveni 45
Atlantis, lost city of 55
Atlantis II 47
atoll 23
Atolla 43

B

bacteria 46–47, 60
barnacle 27, 38, 55, 58; goose 38
barracuda 28
bathysphere 53
bends, the 48
Bermuda Triangle 55
bird, sea 28–29, 38, 40, 62
bivalve 34–35
blue-striped snapper 36
Botticelli, Sandro 16
Branchiocerianthus imperator 11
breeze, sea 12
brittle star 6, 10, 45
bryozoan 6, 23
buoy, monitoring 13
butterfly blenny 18

C

cable, underwater 44, 52
cephalopod 32, 37
Challenger, HMS 11, 45, 52
Chelonia mydas 39
clam 16–17, 24–25, 30, 32, 34, 46–47, 58–59; sand gaper 17
climate 12–13, 26
coastal waters 14–15, 18
cockle, heart 62
cod 26, 57
Continental drift 7; Shelf 8–10, 14, 57; Slope 8–10
copepod 27
coral 7, 10, 20, 22–25, 53–54, 62–63; black 22; brain 23; fire 22; gorgonian 23, 25; hydro- 22; organ-pipe 23; polyp 22–23; reef 22–25, 29, 53–54, 62; rose 23
Coriolis Force 12
crab 16–18, 20–21, 26–27, 30–31; hermit 30–31; masked 17; pea 21; spider 21
crinoid 7
crustacean 18, 30, 38, 58
current 12, 38

D E

Darwin, Charles 23
dead man's fingers 20
decompression 48, 61
Deep Star 53
defence 30–33
diatom 26
dinoflagellate 26
diver 48–49, 53, 61
diving bell 48; suit 49, 61
dolphin 26–27, 36–37; bottlenose 37
Dreadnought, HMS 51
dugong 16, 28
earthquake 45
echinoderm 10, 19, 25
eel 38, 42; gulper 10, 42
Euplectellua spergillium 45
exploration, underwater 52–53

F G

feather star 7, 19
fish, angler- 10, 28, 43; clown 24; craw- 18; cuttle- 30, 32, 34; deep-sea 42–43; emperor angel- 25; flat 14; flying 10, 36; hatchet 10, 40–41; lancet 40–41; lantern 40, 43; lion- 32; puffer 57; rat-tail 10; red band 16; sargassum 30; stone- 32; tripod 10; viper 40; weever 14
fishing 56–58, 62
flounder 14
food chain 26–29
fossil 6–7; fuel 60–61
Gigantura 42
GLORIA 52–53
Great Barrier Reef 23, 25
Gulf Stream 12

H I J

Halley, Edmund 48
herring 26
hurricane 12
hydroid 21; giant 11
ice 11; giant 11; pack 11
iceberg 11, 54
jellyfish 20, 22, 28, 32–33, 41, 43, 58, 62; box 33; glass 41
jet propulsion 34–35

K L

kelp 11, 20–21
Kraken 34
lagoon, formation of 23
lateral lines 42
laver 58
leafy sea dragon 8
Leptocephalus 38
lettuce slug 24–25
light organs 40–42
lobster 18–19, 27, 58; spiny 18
lumpsucker 20

M

mackerel 10, 27
maerl 32
man-of-war 10, 38
Mariana Trench 8–9, 47, 53
Melanocetus 43
Mid-Atlantic Ridge 9, 46–47
Mir 47, 54
mollusc 10, 34, 58
monster, sea 19, 33–34, 42
mother-of-pearl 58–59
mussel 20–21, 33, 58–59; date 25; horse 21, 33

N O

Nautile 47, 54–55
nautilus 36–37, 62–63
Neptune 9
Newt suit 61
Nimbus 7 26
Niño, El 12
oarweed 10, 33
Ocean, Arctic 8; Atlantic 7–9, 13–14, 26, 30; Indian 7–8, 24; Pacific 8, 11–12, 20, 24, 46; Southern 8
octopus 10, 32, 34–35, 58; blue-ringed 32
oil and gas 60–62
Opisthoproctus 41
orange sea fan 22
oyster 58–59

P R

Palaeocoma 6
Pangaea 7
Panthalassa 7
pearl 59
Persian Gulf 60
Piccard, Jacques 53
piddock 18
plankton 12, 22–23, 26–28; phytoplankton 26; zooplankton 26–27
plant 10, 16, 26
plate, crustal 9, 46; Caribbean 9; North American 9
Plateau, Guiana 8
plesiosaur 7
pollution 24, 62
prawn 27, 58
predator 14, 26–27, 30–33, 57
pycnogonid 44
ray 16–17, 27, 33, 36–37; blue-spotted 33; eagle 16–17; electric 36–37; manta 36
reptile 7
rock 18–20, 46, 60

S

salmon 38, 56–57
salmon farming 56
salt 8–9, 11, 59; farms 59
scallop 34–35; queen 23
Scotoplanes 44
scuba diving 48, 50, 52–53
Sea, Arabian 8; Baltic 8; Bering 8; Caribbean 8–9; Coral 8; Dead 9; Mediterranean 8, 55; North 60; Red 8, 25, 50, 53, 63; Sargasso 8, 30, 38; Tasman 8; Tethys 7
sea 8–9; bed 16–17, 44–45, 54–55; cucumber 10, 19, 25, 44, 58; fan 22–23, 28; fir 11, 20–21; grass 10, 16, 28; lily 7, 19, 44–45; mat 20, 29; mouse 7; otter 11, 20, 62; pen 10, 16, 23, 45; potato 17; slug 20, 24–25; snail 30, 47, 58–59; snake 7; spider 10, 44; urchin 11, 18–19, 29, 58; wasp 33
seahorse 17
seal 36, 38; harbour 36; Weddell 36
seaweed 14, 20–21, 28–29, 30, 58
sediment 9, 54
shark 10–11, 27–29, 53, 62; basking 29; blue 28; cat 10–11; great white 62; Greenland 10; hammerhead 53; tiger 29; whale 26
shell 30–33, 58–59, 62–63; carrier 31; gaping file 32–33; noble pen 59
Shinkai 2000 11
shipwreck 54–55
shrimp 47, 58
Siebe, Augustus 49
siphonophore 38, 41
slate-pencil urchin 58
smoker, black 46–47
snorkelling 50, 53
sockeye salmon 57
sonar location 27, 50, 52, 56
sponge 10, 44–45, 48, 54, 58, 63; basket 63; glass-rope 44; Venus flower-basket 10, 45
squid 10, 32, 34, 40, 58
starfish 10, 18–19, 25; Bloody Henry 10; crown-of-thorns 25
Sternoptyx 41
submarine 50–51
submersible 46–47, 50–55
sunstar 10; purple 19

T U V

temperature 8, 10, 13
tidal waves 45
tides 10
Titanic 54
Tolossa 55
Torpedo nobiliana 36
trade winds 12
trawler, fishing 57
treasure 54–55
trenches 8–10, 47, 53
trilobite 7
tsunami 45
Turtle 50
turtle 7, 10, 32, 38–39, 62; green 39
typhoon 12
underwater exploration 48–54
Urashima Taro 39
vents 46–47; Galapagos 47
volcano 9, 23, 45–46

W Z

water spout 12
wave 12–13, 45
weather 12–13
whale 10, 26–28, 36–38, 40, 51, 62–63; blue 26; humpback 28, 38; killer 27; oil 59; sperm 10, 36, 40, 51
whipnose 42
wind 12–13
Wiwaxia 6
wolfish 28
worm 10, 31, 55; bristle 14; parchment 15; peacock 14–15; peanut 14; tube 47
zone, dark 10, 42–43; fracture 9; sunlit 10; twilight 10, 40–41

Acknowledgements

Dorling Kindersley would like to thank:
For their invaluable assistance during photography: The University Marine Biological Station, Scotland, especially Prof. John Davenport, David Murden, Bobbie Wilkie, Donald Patrick, Phil Lonsdale, Ken Cameron, Dr. Jason Hall-Spencer, Simon Thurston, Steve Parker, Geordie Campbell, and Helen Thirlwall. Sea Life Centres (UK), especially Robin James, David Copp, Patrick van der Merwe, and Ian Shaw (Weymouth); and Marcus Goodsir (Portsmouth). Colin Pelton, Peter Hunter, Dr. Brian Bett, and Mike Conquer of the Institute of Oceanographic Sciences. Tim Parmenter, Simon Caslaw, and Paul Ruddock of the Natural History Museum, London. Margaret Bidmead of the Royal Navy Submarine Museum, Gosport. IFREMER for their kind permission to photograph the model of *Nautile*.

David Fowler of Deep Sea Adventure. Mark Graham, Andrew and Richard Pierson of Otterferry Salmon Ltd. Bob Donaldson of Angus Modelmakers. Sally Rose for additional research. Kathy Lockley for providing props. Helena Spiteri, Djinn von Noorden, Susan St. Louis, Ivan Finnegan, Joe Hoyle, Mark Haygarth, and David Pickering for editorial and design assistance.

Extra photography: Ray Möller, Steve Gorton

Model makers: Peter Griffiths and David Donkin

Artwork: John Woodcock and Simone End

Index: Hilary Bird

Picture credits
(l=left r=right t=top b=below c=centre a=above)
American Museum of Natural History 11tl (no. 419(2)).
Heather Angel 38bc.
Ardea / Val Taylor 62tl.
Tracey Bowden / Pedro Borrell 55tc.
Bridgeman Art Library / Prado, Madrid 9tr; Uffizi Gallery, Florence: 16tr.
British Museum 54tr.
Cable & Wireless Archive 44tr.
Bruce Coleman Ltd / Carl Roessler 22c; Frieder Sauer 26tr; Charles & Sandra Hood 27tc; Jeff Foott 28tr, 56tr; Jane Burton 38bl; Michael Roggo 57 tl; Orion Service & Trading Co. 58br; Atlantide SDF 59tr; Nancy Sefton 63br.
Steven J. Cooling 61tr.
Mary Evans Picture Library 11tr, 12tr, 19tl, 20tl, 28tl, 33tr, 34tr, 40cl, 45tr, 48tr, 49tl, 50bl, 52tr, 54c, 60tl.
Ronald Grant Archive 42cl, 55bl.
Robert Harding Picture Library 25tl, 32tr, 32bc, 39br, 57tr, 63tl.
Institute of Oceanographic Sciences 46lc.
© Japanese Meteorological Agency / Meteorological Office 12l.

Frank Lane Photo Agency / M. Newman 11br.
Simon Conway Morris 6tr.
N.H.P.A. / Agence Natur 44c.
Oxford Scientific Films / Toi de Roy 29tr; Fred Bavendam 43tl.
Planet Earth Pictures / Peter Scoones 9tl; Norbert Wu 10–11c, 20cl, 40tr, 40tl, 41l, 42tr; Gary Bell 23br, 55tr; Mark Conlin 25c, 36br; Menuhin 29tc; Ken Lucas 30tl; Neville Coleman 33cr; Steve Bloom 37c; Andrew Mounter 38br; Larry Madin 43br; Ken Vaughan 51cr; Georgette Doowma 63cr.
Science Photo Library / Dr. G. Feldman 26bl; Ron Church 53cr; Simon Fraser 62bl.
Frank Spooner Pictures 47tr, 47cr, 54br, 54bl, 60tr, 60c.
Tony Stone Images, Jeff Rotman 53lc.
Stolt Comex Seaway Ltd 61l.
Town Docks Museum, Hull 63tr.
ZEFA 36cl, 56ct.
Every effort has been made to trace the copyright holders of photographs. The publishers apologize for any omissions and will amend further editions.